Calvin Inclined

A Conversation about Calvinism

ANTHONY DEAN

WestBow
PRESS
A DIVISION OF THOMAS NELSON

WestBow Press books may be ordered through booksellers or by contacting:

WestBow Press
A Division of Thomas Nelson
1663 Liberty Drive
Bloomington, IN 47403
www.westbowpress.com
1-(866) 928-1240

ISBN: 978-1-4497-6150-9 (sc)
ISBN: 978-1-4497-6151-6 (hc)
ISBN: 978-1-4497-6149-3 (e)

Library of Congress Control Number: 2012914083

Printed in the United States of America

WestBow Press rev. date: 10/08/2012

Acknowledgments

I would like to give glory to the Lord for bringing an unknown salesman into my life one day, a man who asked me a pivotal question: "How sovereign is your God?" Thank you, Lord, and thanks to the unknown salesman.

I would also like to express my deepest appreciation to Dr. Tommy Nelson of Denton Bible Church. Dr. Nelson took the time from his church of thousands to meet with me, a pastor of one hundred, to discuss the topic of church growth. Yet, during the conversation, he asked me the same question as the unknown salesman had and challenged me to find the truth of that question. It changed my life forever. Dr. Nelson, I will be forever grateful!

Contents

The year was 1986. I was looking at suits in a local clothing establishment in Tyler, Texas, when a salesman and I began a conversation. During the exchange, I told him I was a preacher and a Southern Baptist at that. He stopped for a moment and then asked a strange question. He said, "How sovereign is your God?" Needless to say, his question caught me by surprise.

I responded, "He is totally sovereign."

His next question stumped me. He said, "Even sovereign in the salvation of a person?"

What was this guy asking? It was a strange way to sell me a suit; however, he kept pressing, and finally, I asked him his purpose in asking these questions. He proceeded to tell me about God's sovereign grace, His electing purposes, and that salvation always begins and ends with God. In short, he told me about his system of theology, better known as Calvinism. I quickly made an excuse that I had to be somewhere else and left the store, embarrassed. Even though I was a recent seminary graduate, I had never heard of Calvinism during my Southern Baptist training, and I didn't want him to know that I didn't know!

When I returned home, I took out my theological dictionary of terms and looked up Calvinism. Basically, it dealt with the doctrine of election. Well, I did hear one sermon on election previously, and I adapted the same viewpoint because I didn't know any better. The preacher came across a text that spoke about election, and his understanding about election was that when he witnessed to a person, he was nominating them for salvation. Then, based on their response, God elected them. At that time, I thought that was a good answer to the doctrine of election. Like most people, I did not want to study the subject. That was doctrine, and people weren't interested in doctrine, or so I thought.

As a result, I didn't preach or talk about the subject; nor was it ever brought up again. It was a dead issue to me. Thus, I concluded that the suit salesman was a little goofy and that I didn't need to engage in doctrinal debates. I needed to bring people to Jesus! Yet, God has a way of bringing back into your life what He wants you to learn. My time was six years later.

Through a series of events, God brought me back to a place where I served as a youth minister some years earlier. This time, I was the senior pastor. After a few short months and the church's gradually growth, I heard about a pastor in a nearby city who had phenomenal growth at his church by transitioning from a traditional Sunday school approach to cell groups. This was an intriguing concept, so I scheduled a lunch with him at a nearby restaurant. The conversation was incredibly helpful, and I learned about his strategy for implementing a cell group structure that I could use in my church. Knowing that I had no other questions for him, I asked the waiter for the check. To my surprise, the pastor asked if we could stay a little longer because he had some questions for me. What in the world could this successful pastor, who was older and had been in the ministry a lot longer than I had, want to know from me? He started the questions by asking me if I had thoroughly read Romans 9. I told him that I had not preached on Romans 9, so I had not studied it thoroughly, even though I had read it many times. He took out his New Testament and read the following verses to me:

> "But it is not as though the word of God has failed. For not all who are descended from Israel belong to Israel, and not all are children of Abraham because they are his offspring, but "Through Isaac shall your offspring be named." This means that it is not the children of the flesh who are the children of God, but the children of the promise are counted as offspring. For this is what the promise said: "About this time next year I will return, and Sarah shall have a son." And not only so, but also when Rebekah had conceived children by one man, our forefather Isaac, though they were not yet born and had done nothing either good or bad—in order that God's purpose of election might continue, not because of works but because of him who calls—she was told, "The

older will serve the younger." As it is written, "Jacob I loved, but Esau I hated."

What shall we say then? Is there injustice on God's part? By no means! For he says to Moses, "I will have mercy on whom I have mercy, and I will have compassion on whom I have compassion." So then it depends not on human will or exertion, but on God, who has mercy." (Romans 9:6-15)

After he finished reading, he began to tell me how he was laying on his couch one day and reading through the ninth chapter and how the truth of God's sovereignty in salvation hit him like ton of bricks. I thought to myself, *Wait a minute . . . I've heard this six years earlier.* In fact, I wanted to ask him if he had ever sold suits! I have to admit that his questions were probing and his grasp of the subject was thorough. He created an interest in me. Now I wanted to at least look into the subject. Before we parted company, he asked if I would do him a favor. He said, "If you are interested in this, which you should be since it is in the Bible, would you do me a favor and pick up R. C. Sproul's book called *Chosen by God?"*

I agreed and told him I would stop by the local bookstore to see if they had it. They did! So, with book in hand, I drove home, read this new book, and began to incline myself toward Calvinism and the doctrine of election. After two years of reading, studying, and listening to arguments for and objections against this great doctrine, I had one of those God-bumps moments. While I was rereading the ninth chapter of Romans along with the first chapter of Ephesians, I was overwhelmed by the grace of God in salvation. To think that God from before the foundation of the world, according to His good pleasure, chose me to be a recipient of His grace was an incredible thought. In fact, why would God want to save anyone when He is not obligated to do so? Why He chooses to save people who constantly rebel against Him is beyond my feeble mind. As I read these great scripture passages, I was so overwhelmed that I began to cry almost uncontrollably. That day, I moved from a person being somewhat inclined toward this new doctrine to a committed Calvinist.

This happened in 1994. Today, in 2012, there is a resurgence in America of people embracing the doctrines of grace, otherwise known as Calvinism. There are even more who are "inclined" to believe them yet do not have a good grasp on the teachings. This book is an attempt to explain the terms and teachings of the doctrines of grace in an easy, understandable way. As a pastor, I found that when people began to ask me about Calvinism, I would often point them to books that helped me along the way. However, when I followed up with them, many didn't take the time to purchase the books or thought they were too hard to grasp. To my delight, when I engaged them in conversation over a period of time, they began to understand and embrace these doctrines. So, the body of this book is written as a conversation between an inquirer and a pastor. It is not meant to be an exhaustive theological treatise but a dialogue. I pray that it would be used by Reformed churches and people alike to give understanding to those who are inquiring about election or those who are inclined to believe these doctrines. It is my hope that those who are "inclined" become an army of the committed. May God bless you in your reading of this conversation concerning these biblical doctrines.

Chapter One

THAT WORD—*ELECTION!*

"There's that word again," said Linden as he and several men from his church were studying the book of Romans at their biweekly Bible study. Over the last two years, eight men from First Community Church had met twice a month early on Tuesday mornings before work to study a book of the Bible, pray, have fellowship, and eat a good breakfast served at the popular Town Cafe.

One of the men looked up from his Bible. "Yes, there it is. So what? We've come across it many times before, and we've always come to the same conclusion."

"Yes, but I think there is more to it than what we've been taught," said Linden.

Most of the men were finishing breakfast, and now their attention was piqued. Alvin, a local businessman and a man of few words, looked across the table at Linden. "What more could there be?"

"Well," said Linden, "let's look at verses ten through eighteen of chapter nine for just a moment." Each man looked quickly at his Bible, and Linden asked Albert if he would read the text to the group.

Albert slid his glasses up on his nose and read out loud the following words:

> "And not only so, but also when Rebekah had conceived children by one man, our forefather Isaac, though they were not yet born and had done nothing either good or bad—in order that God's purpose of election might continue, not because of works but because of him who calls—she was told, "The older will serve the younger." As it is written,

"Jacob have I loved, but Esau I have hated." What shall we say then? Is there injustice on God's part? By no means! For He says to Moses, "I will have mercy on whom I have mercy, and I will have compassion on whom I have compassion." So then it depends not on human will or exertion, but on God who has mercy. For the Scripture says to Pharaoh, "For this very purpose I have raised you up, that I might show my power in you, and that my name might be proclaimed in all the earth." So then he has mercy on whomever he wills, and he hardens whomever he wills." (Romans 9:10-18)

Linden then asked the men to look closely at the words *"in order that God's purpose in election might stand."* He said, "It seems that God has a purpose in election before people are born. But notice the last sentence, 'So then He has mercy on whomever He wills and He hardens whomever He wills.' That seems to say that God is the one doing the choosing and has done so before anyone was born.

"But I was taught something totally different, which was that God saw who would have faith and who wouldn't have faith. Therefore, He chose them based on what He saw in them. Yet according to these verses, God does the choosing instead of seeing that we will have faith at some time in the future. Is that what you guys see?"

The men sat back in their chairs, each pondering what Linden had said. After a short silence, William, one of the older gentlemen of the group, said, "Men, I have been taught what Linden has been taught. The Bible tells us we must have faith in Christ and what He has done in order to be a Christian. That means that a person, once he hears the gospel, must decide if he has enough faith to believe what the gospel says. That involves using our free will to choose whether or not we will believe in what Christ did for us. Therefore, God grants us free will. If He is the one who chooses, what does that do to man's free will?"

"I don't have that answer," remarked Linden. "But the verse does say that God has mercy on whomever He wills."

Albert asked, "Linden, doesn't God have the power to see everything?"

"Well, yes, He does," responded Linden.

"Then can't He see who will have faith and who won't?"

"I'm sure He can, but the question still remains as to whether or not God does the choosing based on His seeing our faith or based on a decision he made before we had faith. The way I see it, I'm inclined to believe that God does the choosing. I just don't understand everything about this word or, excuse me, what the doctrine of election means. But I would like to explore it a little more with you men."

Joe was squirming in his seat as Linden was speaking. He had been down this path before and was a little hesitant. "May I say something, guys?"

"Of course you can. We want to hear from everyone when we meet," stated Linden.

Joe cleared his throat. "Men, I know this word *election* is in the Bible, and I have read this passage many times. I have seen Christians divide over this issue, and I have seen people with differing views get pretty un-Christian with each other. In fact, I have seen things get downright ugly! I would rather just leave it alone and let the chips fall where they may. Only God knows about this election stuff, so it's better that we leave it to Him."

Dennis, a relatively new Christian of about two years, responded quickly. "I know I am new at this discipleship thing, but didn't you guys teach me that if something is in the Bible and is repeated often enough, it must be important?"

Paul and Juan looked at each other with wry smiles, as they had been the ones who had first taken Dennis under their wings and taught him the basics of Bible study and prayer after he had become a Christian.

Juan replied, "He's right. Election is mentioned several times in the Bible. Even Jesus mentions the word. So if it is there, we need to find out the meaning of the word, whether it's controversial or not."

Paul chimed in, "I know I have been taught about election, but previous to that, I had been taught as most of you guys have been. Yet the word is there, and if we are going to live up to our commitment that we made when we started this group—that we would look honestly at the Word and deal with the hard passages when they arise—then we ought to do it."

Everyone nodded, even though some did so with caution.

Linden, sensing some uneasiness, made a suggestion. "Since most of us come to this passage or this doctrine with limited knowledge, with your permission, I would like to ask one of our local pastors what he believes about election, and then I would like to bring my findings back to the group. Would that be okay?" First Community had been without a pastor for some time, and Linden wanted to question someone who had some theological training concerning the subject. He had a particular pastor in mind when he framed the question to his group.

"I think that is a good idea," said Alvin.

"Do you others agree?" asked Linden.

They all nodded.

"Well then, let's all agree that we will approach the subject with open minds, open hearts, and with the attitude that we will not fight about it but accept what the Bible has to say about it."

After everyone agreed, Linden closed the meeting with a prayer and asked the waitress for their checks.

As they were walking out of the Town Cafe, Joe slapped Linden on the back. "Do we know what we are getting into?"

"Well, it should be interesting, to say the least." With that, Linden got into his car. As he turned the key in the ignition, he thought, *Just what are we getting into?*

Chapter Two

HOW SOVEREIGN IS YOUR GOD?

The ringing phone broke the concentration of Kathy Mills, the church secretary at Sovereign Bible Church, as she busily entered calendar requests on her office computer. On the other end of the line was Linden, who was carrying through with his assignment. After he introduced himself, Linden asked if he could speak to Pastor John Martin.

"May I ask about the nature of your call?"

"Well, this may sound a little strange," Linden replied. "But I wanted to talk with him concerning his beliefs about the doctrine of election. I heard from other believers in town that Pastor Martin adheres to this doctrine, and a group of men I meet with on a regular basis want to explore the meaning of this doctrine. I know he's a busy man and may not even be interested in talking with—"

"Oh, not at all! Pastor Martin will be more than happy to talk with you once I tell him why you are calling. Let me get him on the phone. Can you hold please?"

Before Linden could answer, he heard music on the other end of the line, signaling that he had been placed on hold. Within seconds, a voice broke the silence. "This is Brother John. How may I help you?" John Martin was the senior pastor of Sovereign Bible Church and had been for about ten years.

Linden introduced himself and exchanged a few pleasantries. Then he began to give the reason for his call. "Pastor Martin—"

"Please call me Brother John, Linden. That's what everyone here at Sovereign calls me." Although he had a doctorate in theological studies, Pastor Martin was never one to flaunt it and never liked being called "Dr. Martin." It sounded too formal for his modest upbringing and "country" background.

"All right," stated Linden. "Brother John, I guess your secretary told you the purpose of my call?"

"Yes, she did, and I am more than happy to meet with you. But let me ask you something, Linden. Are you ready for this?"

Linden was a little surprised at the question just posed to him by Bro. John. "Is there something I need to be brace myself for?" asked Linden.

"Well, this doctrine, when first encountered, will thrust your mind into convulsions if you're not careful," quipped Bro. John. "Then if you fully embrace them, they will absolutely change your life. If you have been raised in a typical evangelical church, this doctrine will turn your formerly held beliefs on their ear. Almost all that you have been taught concerning salvation will undergo scrutiny. You will question whether you are one of the elect. You will even have doubts and fears. However, if you embrace this doctrine, you will develop a deep sense of humility, gratitude, and perhaps an experience of being born anew for the first time. Grace will take on a new meaning, and you will see God and His sovereignty in a whole new way. Your Christian life will, or let me say, can never be the same. That's why I am asking if you are ready for this."

"Wow." That was the only word Linden could think of at the time. After a short pause, Linden replied, "I guess I'm ready."

"Linden, I don't want to sound harsh or mean, but you need to know, and I need to know you are ready, not just guessing you're ready."

"It's that serious?" asked Linden.

"Yes, it is," replied Bro. John. "This teaching, if truly embraced, will change your life. Trust me, I have lived the change and know the consequences. Some of these changes are fantastic, while others, sadly, are not so great from man's perspective. Have I aroused your interests yet?"

"You certainly have," said Linden. "I would like to know about the 'not so great' things you just mentioned."

"We will get to that in time, but first, let's concentrate on what the doctrine teaches," said Bro. John. "Are you ready?"

"Yes," said Linden. "Let's do this."

"Good, meet me Saturday morning at 7:00 a.m. at the Town Cafe. And before we meet, I need you to look up a few scripture passages. Do you have something to write on?" asked Bro. John.

"Yes, go ahead."

"Look up the following. Let me know if I am going too fast. Please read Isaiah 46:9-10, Psalm 115:3, Job 23:13, 2 Chronicles 20:6, and Romans 9:9-16."

"I believe I have them all, Bro. John," said Linden.

"Good," said the pastor. "I will see you Saturday to start our first topic of discussion on the sovereignty of God."

"But I thought we were going to discuss the topic of election," replied Linden.

"We are, but we need to know or I need to know, first of all, how sovereign your God is, Linden?"

Chapter Three

THE FIRST MEETING

The parking lot at the Town Cafe was almost three quarters full. As Linden found one of the few parking spaces left, he couldn't help wondering what so many people were doing up so early on a Saturday at the Town Cafe! His Bible study group met before work during the early morning hours on a weekday, but because they had to be up anyway to go to work, he completely understood the early hour. But on a Saturday?

As he entered through the doors, he quickly glanced around to see if anyone was waiting for him in the receiving area of the cafe. When he noticed that no one was there, he looked out over the crowd to see if he could see any tables that had only one person seated. Perhaps then he would know it was Bro. John. However, to his dismay, there were three. As he contemplated whether or not to disturb each table by asking the person seated if he happened to be John Martin, the hostess, recognizing Linden from his frequent meetings at the cafe, promptly asked if she could help.

"Yes," said Linden. "I am looking for John Martin. Do you know him?"

"Bro. John?" said the hostess. "Yes, I know him. He's my pastor," she stated as she smiled broadly. "And he happens to be waiting for you in the last booth on the left."

Linden looked quickly at his watch and noticed that it was five minutes until seven. "Has he been here long?" he asked as the hostess escorted him to his destination.

"Oh, he's here every Saturday morning at about six," said the hostess.

Linden thought to himself, *Six a.m. on a Saturday?* As they approached the booth, the hostess turned to Linden, smiled, and said, "Sir, this is my pastor, Bro. John."

Bro. John began to slide out of the booth to introduce himself, but Linden quickly extended his hand to shake his and said, "Please, don't get up. I will slide right in and make myself comfortable."

After an exchange of "how do you do's" and after the waitress poured Linden a cup of coffee and refreshed Bro. John's, Linden could not help but ask the question that was on his mind. "The hostess tells me you arrive every Saturday at 6:00 a.m. Is that true?"

Bro. John smiled and said, "Yes, that's true. We have several men from our church who meet here regularly for study, fellowship, accountability, and prayer. In fact, the table by the window just to our left has some of our men, and three booths down has some. They are praying for you as we speak."

Linden raised an eyebrow and said, "They know we are meeting?"

"Yes," replied the pastor. "These men are the results of an accountability group that I started with them when I first started my pastorate. We met early on a Saturday morning because I wanted to know if their desire and commitment to follow the Lord was as strong as they said it was. As you see, they are meeting with others now and have been doing so over the years to help them in the areas of accountability and discipleship like I helped them. That was one of the requirements that we had. They were to find others to disciple once I sensed they were ready to disciple others. We started with the men in our church but asked them to move beyond the walls of our church by witnessing to those who they knew needed a savior, and some of the discipleship groups are for new believers. In fact, the booth and the table are not the only ones here from our church. We have several small groups going on while we speak. Most of them started with me in the same way you are doing today. I come early not only to fellowship with them, but they know it is still a continuing accountability that we have with each other, making sure that we are 'giving away' what we received. Since they were here, I went around to their tables, enjoyed a little fellowship with them, and asked them to pray for our conversation. They know you are an 'inquirer' into the doctrines of grace."

"Doctrines of grace?" interrupted Linden.

"Oh, yes, forgive me," replied Bro. John. "That's what we call the theological system of election. There are five distinct teachings that we believe that make up what many call the doctrines of grace. We will discuss them as we continue to meet. I informed our groups today of your interest so they could pray for us more specifically."

Needless to say, Linden was impressed with the commitment of so many. Yet he was intrigued at the same time because of what Bro. John had said. "You mean . . . that most of these men were 'inquirers' as you called them, concerning the doctrine of election? Didn't your church already embrace that doctrine?" asked Linden inquisitively.

"No, they didn't," stated Bro. John. "At the outset of my interviewing to come to Sovereign Bible Church as their Senior Pastor, I told them of my beliefs and convictions concerning these doctrines. Most of them agreed that it would be okay since most of them never really knew much about it, and it probably would line up with what they believed anyway. Do you remember how I said that if you embraced these doctrines, they would change your life?"

"Yes, I do," said Linden. "Did it change theirs?"

"You bet," said Bro. John rather emphatically. "Some for the good, others—" Bro. John hesitated for a moment and then said, "I will get to that later. Did you happen to review the verses I gave you?"

"Yes, I did, and I even wrote them down on three-by-five index cards and have them with me," said Linden.

"Great!" exclaimed Bro. John. "Let's talk about God's sovereignty."

Chapter Four

GOD'S SOVEREIGNTY

After they ordered breakfast and conversed about each other, their backgrounds, family, and other matters, Bro. John asked Linden to get out his three-by-five cards with the verses that he had given him during their initial phone call. As Linden placed them on the table, Br. John said, "Linden, the sovereignty of God is a deep subject but one that needs to be understood in its basic form to begin a discussion concerning the doctrine of election. Sovereignty means that God rules. He is the King, the ruler of the universe, and what He says goes. If He is the ruler of all things, which He is, then He rules also over the salvation of men. That's why it is important to understand His sovereign role in the election of His children to salvation. So, let me ask you, if you would, to find the card on which you wrote Psalm 115:3."

Linden skimmed through the cards and found the particular card. "Here it is," stated Linden.

"Good," said Bro. John. "Would you read it for me?"

"Sure thing," responded Linden. "It says,

> "Our God is in the heavens; He does all that He pleases."
> (Psalm 115:3)

"According to this verse, what does God do, Linden?" asked Bro. John.

"Well," replied Linden, "it says God does what pleases Him. Am I correct?" he asked.

"You are indeed correct," said Bro. John. "God does what pleases Him, for there is none higher to please. He is the highest, the most supreme one. To put it in memorable terms,

'God does as He pleases, only as He pleases and always as He pleases.'

You should also have the verse from Job 23:13 on hand. Can you read that one also?"

"Of course," said Linden. As he found the card, he adjusted his glasses and read out loud,

> *"But He is unique, and who can make Him change? And whatever His soul desires, that He does." (Job 23:13)*

Linden looked up from the card and said, "I believe you are going to ask me what God does."

"As a matter of fact, yes, I was," said Bro. John laughingly.

"Well, according to this verse, God does whatever His soul desires," stated Linden.

"That's right, Linden, whatever God's soul desires," replied Bro. John. "And what do you think His soul desires? The answers are found in the next couple of verses that I want you to read to me from your three-by-five cards. Find Isaiah 46:9-10 and 2 Chronicles 20:6 and let's hear them please."

Linden found the verses and read them in order that the pastor asked:

> *"Remember the former things of old; for I am God and there is no other; I am God and there is none like me declaring the end from the beginning and from ancient times things not yet done, saying, 'My counsel will stand, and I will accomplish all my purpose." (Isaiah 46:9-10)*

"Good," said the pastor. "Now read the other verse please."
So Linden read,

"O Lord, God of our fathers, are you not God in heaven? You rule over all the kingdoms of the nations. In your hand are power and might, so that none is able to withstand you."
(2 Chronicles 20:6)

"Thank you, sir!" said Bro John as he took a sip of his coffee and then placed it in front of him on the table. "Please notice, Linden, that the desire of God is to do what according to Isaiah 46:9-10?"

Linden looked over the verse again and focused in on the last part of verse 10. After a moment of thought, he said, "I believe that His desire is His counsel and the accomplishment of His purposes. Am I close?" asked Linden.

"You are correct," replied Bro. John. "Now if you couple this with verse six of 2 Chronicles 20, you will understand that God, the Sovereign One, rules over all the nations. Nations are made of individuals. Since this is so, God rules and accomplishes His purposes in the lives of individuals, nations, and over all things. Nothing can thwart the purposes and plans of God, not even man. Everything we know about anything, everything that has been created, is all under the rule and reign of God the Father. The Bible tells us that He exercises His sovereignty in ordaining all that happens, including those things we think are 'chance,' the actions of good and wicked people, and even the actions of animals. He has established His counsel and purpose, and it will happen. With this in mind, look at your index card that has Romans 9:9-16 on it and read it carefully to yourself and then to me, if you would."

Linden took the card and read silently before he read the verses aloud. As he read, his mind began processing what Bro. John had just told him as it related to God's purposes. About halfway through the verses, Linden quickly looked up from reading to meet Bro. John's eyes and stared silently.

"I suppose you just had an insight, Linden?" asked Bro. John.

"Yes, I did," responded Linden with a look that clearly indicated that he had just connected the dots!

"Why don't you read it aloud and then share with me your insight?" stated Bro. John.

Linden held the card in front of him and read the following:

> *"For this is what the promise said: "About this time next year I will return and Sarah will have a son." And not only so, but also when Rebekah had conceived children by one man, our forefather Isaac, though they were not yet born and had done nothing either good or bad—in order that God's purpose in election might continue, not because of works but because of him who calls—she was told, "The older will serve the younger." As it is written, "Jacob have I loved, but Esau I hated." (Romans 9:9-12)*

"Bro. John, I know I haven't finished the passage, but can I share with you my insight because it concerns the eleventh and twelfth verses, if you don't mind?" Linden requested.

"Sure, go ahead," responded Bro. John.

Linden looked down at the verses and then again at Bro. John, and as he did, he said, "According to what we just discussed concerning God accomplishing His purposes and that nothing can withstand the purpose of God, then when God purposed election, that which He purposed in election will be accomplished because God does what He has purposed." Linden queried, "Am I on the right track?"

"Yes, you are, Linden," acknowledged Bro. John. "But I need you to continue reading so you can see what it means by election and how God's sovereignty relates to it. So, please continue with the rest of the verses," Bro. John said.

Linden continued reading the verses:

> *"What shall we say the? Is there injustice on God's part? By no means! For He says to Moses, "I will have mercy on whom I will have mercy, and I will have compassion on whom I will have compassion." So then it depends not on human will or exertion, but on God who has mercy." (Romans 9: 14-16)*

After the reading of the verse, Bro. John remarked, "Linden, the main point of our conversation this morning is to see from the Scripture that God is sovereign and from the beginning has a counsel or purpose that He will fulfill. That even includes the salvation of man because what you just read says that 'I will have mercy on whom I have mercy, and I will have compassion on whom I have compassion.' Thus, as you just read, He had a purpose in choosing Jacob and not Esau to fulfill the purpose of election and He has the sovereign right to do so because He rules over all, even man."

As the pastor finished his statement, the look on Linden's face conveyed to Bro. John that not only were the wheels churning in his mind but that there was a hint of confusion. Bro. John responded to the look of confusion by saying, "Linden, something is going on in your mind because it is written all over your face. Want to share?" asked Bro. John.

"Yes I do," responded Linden. "Pastor, you say that God is sovereign over the salvation of men by accomplishing His purpose through election. But I have always been taught that man has a free will, that God never violates the free will of man and God allows man to choose or reject the offer of salvation. This purpose of election that you speak of doesn't make sense to me, especially if we have the will to choose."

As soon as Linden finished his sentence, the waitress arrived at their table with their food. As he looked over the food before them and then looked at Linden, Bro John responded with a smile, "Linden, it's great that you are weighing this against what you have been taught, for I told you at the beginning that this doctrine will throw your mind into convulsions. For the moment, however, let me pray and give God thanks for our meal. And we will continue our conversation, and I will hopefully clear up some of the confusion . . . eventually."

"Eventually?" asked Linden.

"Patience, my friend," replied Bro. John. "This is just the beginning of many Saturday morning meetings!"

Chapter Five

GOD IS NOT OBLIGATED

After he gave thanks and while he poured hot maple syrup over his pancakes, Bro. John began the conversation once again. "Linden, you stated that you have been taught that man has a free will, and indeed, it is correct that he does. But I want you to know that I will respond to that next week."

"Next week?" remarked Linden with an apprehensive smile.

"Yes, next week," said Bro. John. "I want us to continue to talk about God's sovereignty and respond to the teaching you received concerning the violation of man's will. Would that be okay?" asked the pastor.

"Of course," replied Linden. "I'm here to learn."

"Good," said Bro. John. "So let me ask you a couple of questions that relates to God's sovereignty. You do understand that God is not a created being but is a personal being, right?" inquired Bro. John.

"Indeed," answered Linden.

As Linden spoke, Bro. John took another sip of coffee and then proceeded with his line of reasoning.

"Since God is a personal being, He is also a supreme being, which means He has supreme freedom and authority to do His will. We established that fact from the scripture we read this morning. Since He is sovereign, meaning that He rules over all and has authority over all, He also has a greater freedom than those who are under His authority. To put it another way, we could say that God is free. I could also say that I am free. Yet if God is sovereign, then His freedom to be God is greater than my freedom as His creature. He can do what He wants, when He wants, and where He wants. If that is so, then when my freedom runs contrary to His freedom to do what He wants with His creatures, I lose. The creature's freedom never restricts the freedom of the sovereign God. If there were any restrictions to God's sovereignty, then He would not be sovereign. When you say that God never violates man's free will, you have just placed a restriction on the sovereignty of God, a restriction, I might add, that is never found in the pages of Scripture. Would you agree with what I have said so far, Linden?" asked Bro. John.

"Well," said Linden, "let me ask you a question before I give you an answer. Do you mean that God would violate the will of man?"

Bro. John spoke up, "Let me answer that question with a question. Is God required to seek a person's permission to do with that person what He pleases? You brought your Bible so turn to the passage we read earlier in Romans 9."

Linden quickly pushed his plate to the side and placed his Bible on the table and then turned to Romans 9.

"Look at verse 19 and following, and if you will, Linden, read it out loud until I tell you to stop," asked Bro. John.

Linden found the verse and began to read the passage:

> "You will say to me then, "Why does he still find fault? For who can resist his will? But who are you, O man, to answer back to God? Will what is molded say to its molder, "Why have you made me like this?" Has the potter no right over the clay, to make out of the same lump one vessel for honorable use and another for dishonorable use?" (Romans 9: 19-21)

"Stop right there, Linden," said Bro. John. "The Apostle Paul knew that he would get this kind of reaction to the statement previously written in the verses preceding verse nineteen concerning the purpose of election. So, he immediately answers their questions before they asked them. Paul states that God has the right to do with His creation what He wants done. So, does He need permission from a sinner to do what He wants to do with that sinner?"

Linden sheepishly replied, "I guess not."

Bro. John, wanting to make his reasoning clear, pressed on with another line of questioning. "Linden," he asked, "do people ask God to place them in the city of their birth before their birth takes place?"

"No," replied Linden, "they don't."

"That's right," remarked Bro. John. "Neither do they select their parents, their brothers or sisters, or their names. They don't even ask to inherit a sinful nature. This has already been determined by God in His sovereignty before they were born. Israel did not ask God to be His chosen nation, but they are. Even if a person from Israel screamed at God and said, 'You have violated my will,' God's plan for choosing Israel is not thwarted just because somebody somewhere in Israel didn't like it. He has the right to determine what He wants, and nothing can thwart it. Israel's destiny as God's chosen nation has been decreed by God. Your birth, where you were born, and to whom you were born was ordained by God from the beginning of time. I know that is hard to understand, but nonetheless, it is true if you believe in the sovereignty of God. Now, since you were born and you did inherit a sinful nature apart from Christ, your eternal destiny has been determined. We all deserve death and hell. In one sense, a person could say, like it says in the verses you just read, 'I didn't get a choice! That is a violation of my will.' If God has restricted Himself by the freedom of the human will, then wouldn't He have to ask a person whether or not he wanted to be born to a certain set of parents or whether they wanted to have a sinful nature? And how could He ask them if they didn't exist? Rather, He, as the creator, established that men left in their fallen state would receive eternal punishment. Since He has decreed that a curse took place when man sinned in the garden, that everyone born has a sinful nature, and that sinful nature separates them from God, is it wrong of God to 'go the extra mile' and ensure the salvation of those whom He has said are His elect even if it means, as you put it, it would violate their wills? Now be careful how you answer that question, Linden, because your answer will let you know if you really believe God is sovereign or not," stated Bro. John.

Linden looked intently at Bro. John, contemplating his answer. After a short silence, which allowed the pastor to take another bite of his breakfast, Linden said, "If I say that man's freedom has been violated, then I run into the problem of man's freedom becoming an obstacle to God being allowed to do what He wants to with His creation. I just don't think that I have that power. However, it just doesn't seem like God would do that."

Bro. John quickly responded, "Linden, it seems that your struggle is with the concept of fairness. I get that answer quite often. People who do not believe that God is absolutely sovereign, even over salvation, like to throw out the fairness concept, believing that God is less loving if He doesn't treat all men equally. Is that where your struggle lies?" asked Bro. John.

"I guess you could say that," said Linden.

"Remember," countered Bro. John, "that God says He will have mercy on whom He will have mercy. Just because He grants mercy to one does not mean that He has to grant mercy to all. We would all prefer that to happen, but I cannot place my preferences above what the scripture teaches. I can prefer that God would save everyone, but I cannot demand that He do so. That would be the height of arrogance on my part. Besides, when you read through the scriptures, you will see God is not treating everyone equally or 'fairly' as some would say. God gave a special status to Israel that He did not give to Babylon. Why did God choose Moses and call him as a special leader of His people yet did not give the same calling to Abdul of the desert? It's because God made a sovereign choice that did not treat people in the same way He treated Israel or Moses. But isn't that His prerogative, being that He is God?" asked Bro. John.

"Yes, sir," replied Linden. "According to the verses we just read, the potter has the right to do with the clay what He wants to do. Man, this viewpoint is really making me think!"

"Didn't I tell you at the outset that this doctrine will shake you up?" asked Bro. John laughingly. "Here's something to really hang your hat on. If God's sovereignty is restricted by a person's freedom, then man has become sovereign and not God. Think about that implication, Linden. If man is sovereign in the case of His salvation, then God would be disappointed every time someone rejects Him and His offer of salvation because He really doesn't have the power to accomplish His purpose in their life because man is in control over his own destiny. Accordingly, God would be up in heaven, pleading with a person, saying, 'Please accept me. Please accept me. It's up to you. Oh, please accept me!' Doesn't that sound a little ridiculous?" asked Bro. John

"When you put it that way, that does seem strange," stated Linden.

"God is not in heaven, begging people to accept Him. He is accomplishing His purpose of election, salvation, and sanctification in the lives of those whom He has granted mercy," replied Bro. John. "Linden, to sum up our conversation, for I think, as they say in the country, 'I have loaded your wagon' enough this morning, God has made sovereign choices since the beginning of time according to His sovereignty and His freedom to do so. I want you to mull these things over this week. Please remember that I am not trying to 'coerce' you to believe these things. I just want you to see what the scripture has to say and to think on these things. So, meditate on this thought: 'God is not obligated to grant mercy to anyone.' God always reserves the right to extend His mercy to whom He wants to extend mercy. Now I want you to prepare for next week by doing two things for me."

"Okay," said Linden, "I have pen in hand."

"First of all, look for examples within our society and within your family that illustrate someone's will overriding someone else's will. I believe that will help you grasp this concept a little better, and you can report your findings to me next week. Second, read the following verses before we meet again: John 1:12-13 and John 6:37-44. We will get into a discussion about free will and if it is really violated in the way some assume today."

"Now wait a minute, pastor," remarked Linden. "After saying that God has every right to do so, are you now saying that He doesn't violate our will?"

Bro. John picked up the check, slid out of his chair, and smiled as he looked down at Linden, who looked rather dumbfounded. "Next week, my friend," said Bro. John. "Next week!"

Chapter Six

TUESDAY MORNING BIBLE STUDY

"Why didn't he just explain the meaning of election instead of getting into the sovereignty of God?" asked Henry as they sat around the table for their Tuesday morning Bible study at the Town Cafe. All the men present fixed their eyes on Linden as he placed his cup of coffee back onto the table.

"Bro. John was setting the foundation for the doctrine of election so the starting point is the sovereignty of God and what it really means," replied Linden. "God's sovereignty over His creation, to do with His creation and His creatures as He wishes, including the salvation of mankind, is a pivotal point because you have to decide if what God says is true in Romans 9 when the Apostle Paul writes that He will have mercy on whom He will have mercy. Bro. John was saying that this is God's sovereign choice to do so and that God always accomplishes what He says He is going to do."

"I know where you are going with this, Linden," protested William. "You are going to say that God does all the choosing of those who get to go to heaven. But doesn't that violate our free will in the matter? Because I know every one of us sitting around this table made a decision to accept Christ. We just didn't wake up one morning and *poof*, we were Christians. God has allowed us the privilege of choosing Him or rejecting Him. It is our choice, not His. He gives us the opportunity to receive Him but never violates our will to receive Him. That would make us mere robots or mere puppets."

"What about that, Linden?" asked Joe. "Are you saying that Bro. John believes we're just puppets and have no choice in what we do at all in our lives?"

"I don't believe he is saying that at all, but that is next week's discussion," replied Linden.

"So he just left you hanging?" asked Alvin. "That can leave you a little confused because just from our conversation this morning, I am already confused!"

Linden looked over his discipleship group and could see that they indeed wanted some answers but could already sense that while some were interested, others already were putting a stake down concerning their beliefs and did not have a sense of openness.

"Men, I don't have all the answers for you at the moment, but in time, I will be able to explain to you what I learn from Bro. John and why he believes like he does," said Linden. "I do want us to remember that we agreed to explore this issue of election and we need to be open-minded to what the scriptures teach about this doctrine and not draw any conclusions so early in our study. I personally have to examine what I believe and have been taught, and quite frankly, some of the things that were said by Bro. John, I have never really thought about."

"Give us an example," said Juan.

"Okay," responded Linden. "In discussing God's sovereignty and how Bro. John stated that God has the right to do with His creatures as He desires, he asked me to think of situations where someone else's will trumped my own will. In reflecting on this, about seven months ago, I was driving to work and made the mistake of looking at my cell phone to get my e-mails. I admit that I was reading an e-mail as I was driving, which is not the safest thing to do. As I was reading and glancing up at the road and then back down to my phone, my mind was preoccupied with the e-mail instead of paying attention to my surroundings. Suddenly, I hear the sound of a siren from behind me. When I looked up, I realized I was smack dab in the middle of a school zone! I was going thirty-two in a twenty-mile-an-hour zone!" The men snickered, made a few condescending remarks, all in good humor, and then asked what happened.

"Well, he ticketed me and gave me a lecture about speeding through a school zone. He stated that I could have endangered many school children as well as myself," said Linden. "The fine was quite hefty, but I am very much aware now when I enter school zones! As I reflected on that event, it was not my will that the police officer give me a ticket. In fact, I let him know that I was not paying attention, should have been, and also explained that in thirty plus years of driving, I have only had one ticket and that was when I was eighteen years old. Nevertheless, he just kept on writing! So, in a sense, you could say that when his will came up against my will, I lost! He had more authority than I did, even though I did not want him to write me that ticket. To make it applicable to what we are studying, if God is all-powerful and does what He pleases, can He not step into our lives and direct us where He wants us to go?" asked Linden.

"Of course He can, but He doesn't violate our will, Linden, so He chooses not to do so," asserted Henry.

"Henry, that is what I have been taught, but I cannot find in the scripture where God gave up the right not to intervene in our lives," declared Linden. "In fact, I did a search on verses related to God's sovereignty and how He rules over all things, and I found a couple of verses that really hammer this home. If you guys would take your Bibles and turn to Proverbs 16."

The men busily turned to the specific chapter, and once Linden saw that everyone was looking at the sixteenth chapter, he asked Paul to read verse one, William to read verse nine, and Dennis to read verse thirty-three. Paul began and read,

> *"The plans of the heart belong to man, but the answer of the tongue is of the Lord". (Proverbs 16:1)*

"William, go ahead and read verse nine," said Linden.

William cleared his throat, pushed up his glasses on his nose, and read,

> *"The heart of a man plans his ways, but the Lord establishes his steps." (Proverbs 16:9)*

After William read his verse, Linden nodded to Dennis and he read,

> *"The lot is cast into the lap, but its every decision is from the Lord." (Proverbs 16:33)*

As soon as Dennis finished reading, Linden said, "Men, these verses clearly teach that even though we are engaged in acts of the will, God is behind the scenes, controlling them to accomplish His purposes. The way I see it, when I plan something according to my will, God steps in to accomplish His will because He has the right to do so and directs or establishes my steps. I believe that is just another way of saying that His will trumps my will because He is free to do so."

"As this relates to salvation, are you saying that as we make the decision to believe in Christ, God is actually making the decision or directing us to make the decision?" asked Albert.

Again, all eyes turned toward Linden. Linden sat back in his chair, took a deep breath, let it out, and said, "Men, let me answer that with a deep theological statement. I don't know!"

Albert, always the one with a quick response, said, "Great! We have the blind leading the blind!"

When the laughter died down, Linden explained his answer. "Men, I really do not have all the answers at this moment. Nor can I promise that I ever will. I do know that the topic of Saturday's discussion with Bro. John is on the very subject of free will and how God either violates our will or He doesn't. He kinda left it up in the air, which really piqued my interest. I just know that it is undeniably clear in the scriptures that God's will always supersedes His creatures' when it comes to accomplishing His will. I will make sure I have a good grasp of what he tells me so I can report back to you. Why don't we pray and bring our time to a close? I know all of you are ready to get to your workplace!"

Linden's last remark was met with the usual banter and humor that characterized the friendship of the group. After they prayed, the men said their good-byes and walked out of the restaurant and toward their cars. As Linden was opening his door, he heard Dennis calling his name and coming toward him. When Dennis was within arm's length of Linden, he asked, "Do you think the pastor would mind if I sat in on your conversation on Saturday? Our discussion today really hit a chord with me."

"I don't see why not, Dennis," said Linden. I will call him before Saturday and let him know you are coming. Just be sure to look over those verses we discussed today, the ones I gave you that Bro. John gave to me, so we can be on the same page. Be there a little before 7:00, and we'll hopefully learn something about free will."

"Great," expressed Dennis. "See you there!"

As Linden drove out of the parking lot and toward his workplace, he silently prayed, "Thank you, Lord, that the teaching today struck a chord with Dennis. I pray that the chord was in tune with you and your teachings and that some didn't tune me out!"

Chapter Seven

OUR STRONGEST INCLINATION

"Excellent analogy, Linden," exclaimed Bro. John after Linden told him about the ticket incidence. As their food was placed on the table before them, Bro. John said, "Now can you imagine going before the judge, him sentencing you to not only pay the fine but spend some time in community service by being the crosswalk guard in that same school zone for two days, yet you protesting and telling the judge that his sentencing violates your free will? What do you think his response would be?"

"Probably the same answer I gave my daughter last night when she was arguing with me about her curfew. I told her that she could protest all she wanted but in the end, my authority was greater than her authority as a child in my home. So, my will overruled hers. I believe the judge would have told me something along those lines and probably some other few choice words!" claimed Linden.

"Another good analogy,' expressed Bro. John. "I believe you are grasping what I believe the scriptures teach concerning God's sovereignty."

"It's becoming clearer, but I still have some questions concerning how His sovereignty relates to free will. I do know that when I brought up this very subject in our Bible study this week, there were some who were as confused as I am on the issue of free will and some who were downright adamant that God still never violates our will," divulged Linden.

"I'm also anxious to hear this discussion, pastor," chimed in Dennis, "because when you answer Linden's questions, I know mine will be answered."

Bro. John was glad that Linden had brought Dennis to their Saturday morning breakfast. Having another set of ears present would help both men clarify what was being discussed if, at a later time, either one of the men might not remember all that had been spoken.

"Let me begin our conversation by asking you men some questions before you ask me your questions," said Bro. John. Both men nodded with approval, and the pastor began his first question. "Linden," said Bro. John, "why did you get an omelet today and not pancakes?"

Linden was somewhat dazed by the question. He wondered what his selection of breakfast items had to do with their discussion of free will but answered reluctantly, "I wanted an omelet today because I need a little more protein in my diet. The eggs and meat inside the omelet will give me what I need instead of the pancakes. Why do you ask?" uttered Linden.

"Patience, my friend" responded Bro. John. When he turned to Dennis, Bro. John proceeded to ask him the same. "Dennis, why did you get oatmeal and fruit?"

Dennis answered, "My doctor told me I had to eat more fiber and whole grains, so oatmeal and fruit it is. I certainly would have rather had the country biscuits with gravy, but doctor's order, you know. Besides, my wife might have a spy in the cafe today, waiting to report my dietary choices."

The men chuckled, made a few comments how their wives knew how to hold them accountable, and jokingly told of the consequences that they had experienced when they didn't hold up their end of the bargain. Bro. John continued his line of questioning. "So for each of you, there was a reason for your decision, am I correct?" asked Bro. John?

Both men nodded in agreement. Bro. John continued, "One wanted protein, and the other wanted to obey doctor's orders. Could either of you have made the breakfast decision without a reason?" inquired Bro. John.

"I guess we could have," responded Dennis. "I could have just left it to whim and made a decision."

"So, you are saying that you could have made a decision without any prior inclination?" asked Bro. John

"Yes," responded Dennis.

"Now I want you both to think about this. If you had no inclination or should I say, you had no prior knowledge of the items on the menu, for to make decisions, we must first have some idea of what we are choosing, then you would sit here and not eat breakfast because there would be no food in front of you," stated Bro. John.

"Wait a minute, pastor," said Linden. "Why would we not be eating?" he asked.

"Let me explain," said Bro. John. "When I speak of using the will to make decisions, I am saying that the decision-making process is nothing more than the mind choosing what it desires. If I am not inclined to any item on the menu or do not have prior knowledge of the menu, I would not choose anything because I do not have a desire to do so. You see, you had a desire for more protein in your diet, and Dennis had a desire for more grains so he could live longer and healthier. No one forced you to make these decisions. They were based on your prior knowledge, experience, motives and values. You had a reason for choosing the way you did. We could call this decision-making process 'free will.' The basic definition of free will is being able to choose according to our desires. Are you grasping this point?" asked Bro. John.

Linden responded, "I think I can sum it up this way: The decisions I make each and every day have a reason or an inclination behind it."

"Absolutely," replied Bro. John emphatically. "Why did you come here today? Was it because you had no inclination or desire to do so, or was there a reason? Why would anyone come to the cafe this morning if they had no reason or inclination? To say that you came for no reason is to conclude that your will was in neutral. If your will was in neutral, then you wouldn't make a choice at all. I believe you had a reason. You wanted to learn, and the desire to learn was greater than your desire to stay at home on a Saturday morning in a nice, warm, cozy bed. With that said, we use our free will to choose what we choose according to the strongest desire at the moment."

"I see," said Dennis. "The strongest inclination for me was to obey the doctor's orders because of the knowledge I have pertaining to my health. If I do not choose to eat right, I cut short the quality of my life. Therefore, I have a desire to live in a more healthy body, so I choose foods that will enhance my health."

"You got it!" exclaimed Bro. John. "How about you, Linden? Does all this make sense?" he asked.

"It does, but I'm still not totally connecting the dots on how this affects the doctrine of election. Maybe I'm just slow or perhaps haven't had enough coffee yet," commented Linden.

Bro. John smiled and said, "Linden, my strongest inclination on choosing my answer to your dilemma of being slow or not having enough coffee is the former!"

The men had a good chuckle and acknowledged that when it came to understanding the concept of free will as it was defined, it could be mind-boggling at times. Yet Linden and Dennis were ready for the next step.

"Bro. John, if we do have free will, then doesn't it mean that we choose Christ based on the knowledge that we receive concerning Him or concerning whether or not we want to go to heaven when we die, especially if that is what we desire?" asked Linden.

"Good question," remarked Bro. John. "Before I answer your question, I would like you both to turn to the scriptures I gave Linden last week. Let's look at John 6:37-44, and if you would, Dennis, please read it aloud."

Dennis quickly found the Gospel of John, the sixth chapter, and read the following:

> "All that the Father gives me will come to me, and whoever comes to me I will never cast out. For I have come down from heaven, not to do my own will but the will of him who sent me. And this is the will of him who sent me, that I should lose nothing of all that he has given me, but raise it up on the last day. For this is the will of my Father, that everyone who looks on the Son and believes in him should have eternal life, and I will raise him up on the last day."
>
> So the Jews grumbled about him, because he said, "I am the bread that came down from heaven." They said, "Is not this Jesus, the son of Joseph, whose father and mother we know? How does he now say, 'I have come down from heaven?'" Jesus answered them, "Do not grumble among yourselves. No one can come to me unless the Father who sent me draws him. And I will raise him up on the last day." (John 6:37-44)

"Guys," continued Bro. John, "these verses contain some great truths that are often overlooked. Looking at verse thirty-seven, it says that the Father gives people to the Son because the "whoever" in this verse are the people whom the Father gives to Jesus. So we see that the Father is giving people to Him for salvation and He will raise them up on the last day. But Jesus throws a monkey wrench in on the process. Even though God gives people to Jesus for salvation, Jesus says that no can come to Him unless the Father draws them. I want you to concentrate on the word 'can.' Would you agree that this simple little word 'can' is a word depicting ability?" inquired the pastor.

"I would agree with that," said Linden.

"I agree also," Dennis chimed in.

"Good," agreed Bro. John as he leaned forward in his chair. "This is a hinge piece for the reformed view of salvation and goes along with your previous question, Linden. If we base our decisions on the strongest desire at the moment, yet Jesus says we cannot come to Him, or should I say, we do not have the ability to choose Him, then how do we get the 'desire' to make a choice?"

"Hang on there, preacher," injected Linden. "I need you to repeat a couple of things. Jesus says that no one can come to Him unless the Father draws them. That is a statement of ability, right?"

"You are right," said Bro. John

Linden continued, "So, if we do not have the ability to come to Christ, then we can't come to Christ."

"Exactly!" exclaimed Bro. John. "You are on the right track."

"But I know I made the choice to believe in Christ," protested Linden.

'Exactly!" exclaimed Bro. John once again.

"Now I'm confused, Bro. John," asserted Dennis.

Bro. John laughed at the expressions on each man's face as they tried to digest what had just been said. "Stay with me on this," uttered Bro. John as he brought his laughter under control. "We just discussed that we base our decisions on our desires. You also know that within our hearts, there is the desire for evil. That evil desire causes us to want to choose that which is evil. Yet in the beginning, it wasn't so. Adam and Eve had desires that were not evil. Their desires were for fellowship with God. They had the ability to choose fellowship with Him. However, when they chose sin over fellowship with God, they lost the ability to choose what is righteous because their nature now was changed. They received a sinful nature. This sinful nature was passed down to every human being who has ever been born and ever will be born. Those who hold to the truths of the doctrines we are discussing believe that when man fell, it affected his whole being, including the will. Since a person's will has been affected, or better yet to say, has been corrupted, now his will is inclined to its evil desires and not for God. The desire for evil is an outgrowth of his nature. It is the nature of a sinful person to sin. It is not his nature to choose God because he does not have a desire for God. While a person still has a free will, that will has been limited in what it can choose because of the sin nature. Now think with me on this. You know that the book of Ephesians says we are dead in our trespasses and sin. In fact, turn to chapter two of Ephesians, and one of you read from verse one through five."

Linden found Ephesians quickly and began to read the verses:

> "And you were dead in your trespasses and sins in which you once walked, following the course of this world, following the prince of the power of the air, the spirit that is now at work in the sons of disobedience—among whom we all once lived in the passions of our flesh, carrying out the desires of the body and mind and were by nature children of wrath, like the rest of mankind." (Ephesians 2:1-3)

Bro. John held up his hand and said, "Stop there for a moment, Linden. Listen carefully to what it says. You were dead. You followed the prince of the power of the air. You lived by the passions of the flesh. You carried out the desires of the body and mind. The reason that mankind does this is because he has a fallen nature that will only carry out the desires of the flesh or, in other words, has only the ability to choose according to his nature. Since man is dead to the things of God, he will not choose God. According to Romans 3, no one even seeks God."

"Is that true?" asked Dennis.

"Why not turn to Romans 3:10-12 and see for yourself?" replied Bro. John.

Dennis thumbed away from Ephesians and found Romans 3. He read,

> "As it is written: 'None is righteous, no, not one; no one understands; no one seeks for God. All have turned aside; together they have become worthless; no one does good, not even one." (Romans 3:10-12)

"Dennis," said Bro. John, "if no one seeks God, then how can they choose God?"

Dennis sat silently for a brief moment and then answered, "I don't see that they would, seeing that they do not have God as one of their strongest desires. Wow! They don't seek God. I never knew that. I thought everyone was seeking God in some form or fashion since we were made in His image."

"Let me put it this way, Dennis. People are seeking the benefits of God or some form of spirituality as they suppose 'being spiritual' to be, but they are not seeking the one true God. Their nature, being dead spiritually, will not choose Him, or should I say as Jesus says, cannot choose Him," responded Bro. John. "They will only choose according to their nature. Since their nature is sinful and they are dead in their trespasses and sins, they cannot choose what they do not desire."

"So, how in the world does anyone come to Christ if they do not have the desire to do so?" asked Linden.

"Glad you asked," said Bro. John as he took another sip of his coffee and placed it in the saucer on the table. "Turn back to Ephesians 2 and complete the two verses where we left off."

Linden found Ephesians 2 once again in his Bible and read,

> "But God, being rich in mercy, because of the great love with which He loved us, even when we were dead in our trespasses, made us alive together with Christ—by grace you have been saved." (Ephesians 2:4-6)

After Linden finished the passage, Bro. John spoke, "Men, if we were dead, then someone had to bring about life in us. God had to do something in us first so that we could respond to Christ since we do not have the ability to choose Him. Here is the dividing line between the reformed view, which I hold, and the non-reformed view. The non-reformed view says that there is something still left in man that has not been affected by the fall, something that will allow him to incline himself to or desire Christ. I call that view 'the somewhat sick' view."

"What?" laughed Linden as he asked the question.

"Well, think of it this way, Linden." replied Bro. John. "If there is something left in man that is untouched by the fall, then we must conclude that Paul really didn't mean that we were dead but somewhat sick. A sick person still has the ability to get up and do a few things or at the least lift his hand or his head off the pillow since he is not dead. He still can respond to something since he is 'somewhat sick' but not dead. That is why I call it 'the somewhat sick' view because it denies that our whole being was corrupted in the fall and is now dead. I believe this view to be a serious departure from the truth presented in scripture. The Apostle Paul emphatically says, 'We are dead in trespasses and sins,' not somewhat sick. The last time I checked, dead people cannot respond to anything. That is why I say that before a person can choose Christ, something has to be done in that person to incline them to desire Christ. If not, then the person himself makes a choice based on their desire for Christ. The question remains then: How were they inclined to choose Christ? How can anyone choose something if they have no desire for that which they choose?"

"Let me see if I understand what you are saying," piped in Dennis. "Before I was a Christian, I was dead to spiritual things because of sin."

"That's correct," answered Bro. John. "Please continue."

"Okay," responded Dennis. "Because of my deadness or unresponsiveness to things of God, God had to cause me to respond by doing something in me."

"Yes, He had to make you alive, which, according to the scriptures we just read, was an act of mercy and grace," said Bro. John. "This 'making alive' is what we call regeneration, or as the term implies, something has to be generated again. That is the meaning of the term. You were dead, so now you have to be generated again or made alive. The reformed view calls this 'making alive' being born again, and it has to happen first so that you can believe. The non-reformed view has an unregenerate person choosing first, which presupposes that there is something left in man that can actually muster up the will to choose Christ."

This time, Linden held up both hands to Bro. John to get him to stop and explain himself. "Wait a minute. Wait just a minute," said Linden. "Don't we believe first and then we are born again?" inquired Linden.

"Again, Linden," asked Bro. John, "how do we choose to be born again if we have no desire for God? There first must be the desire. Since it is not there, God, in His wonderful love, mercy, and grace, changes our hearts so that we now desire Christ. That has to happen first, or we would never choose Christ. He grants us this gift of grace so that we can believe."

"Okay, I think I have it!" exclaimed Dennis. "Let me see if I can explain it. Man is dead in sin, so he cannot choose Christ. God causes Him, by a supernatural act, to be born again, thus changing his heart. When his heart changes, he will choose Christ because he now desires Christ. Is that right?" asked Dennis hesitantly.

"Absolutely correct!" stated Bro. John decisively. "Now here is what I meant earlier, Linden, when you said you chose Christ and I said you indeed did. God didn't choose Christ for you, or rather, He did not believe for us. When He regenerates someone or makes them alive, they now can make a choice for Christ. Previous to new birth, according to their nature, they could not. Now they can or have the desire for Christ because God has planted a desire in their hearts for Christ. Now since they desire Christ, they exercise their newly opened will or newly enlightened heart to make a choice through faith. Indeed, it is their faith, but it is a faith that has been granted to them by God. That's why the passage in Ephesians 2:8-9 is so precious to the believer. It says,

> "For by grace you have been saved through faith. And this is not your own doing, it is a gift from God, not as a result of works, so that no one can boast.'" (Ephesians 2: 8-9)

"So, grace is a gift, and so is the faith to believe. Now it is your faith that believes, but it is a faith that did not begin with us. It came from God. That is what is so marvelous about the grace of God and is so humbling at the same time. When you were dead in trespasses and sins, God, who chose you from before the foundation of the earth, granted you grace and faith, even when you didn't deserve it," concluded Bro. John.

Both men sat back in their chairs and looked intently at the pastor as to suggest they were deep in thought. Bro. John responded likewise and sat back in his chair while he brought his cup of coffee to his lips to take one final sip. As he placed his cup onto the table, he asked jokingly, "Wagons loaded?"

"So heavy the wheels are creakin' and the horses are strugglin'," replied Linden playfully.

"Well, I suppose that is enough for today, men. You have enough to chew on for the week, so is next Saturday still good for you guys?" queried Bro. John.

Both Dennis and Linden nodded in the affirmative.

"All right then," said Bro. John, "here is your next assignment. Since we have looked at the sovereignty of God and realized that God has mercy on whom He will have mercy and He accomplishes all that He desires, and knowing now that God has to act upon the heart to change it so it will desire Christ because of our deadness to spiritual things, to whom does this apply? Come back with some scriptures that talk about believing in Jesus, receiving Jesus, passages that say for whom Christ dies, passages that use the word 'chosen' and any other scripture that relates to salvation, and we will begin our discussion about election. You think your wagon is loaded now? Wait until next week!"

"I'll be sure to take my aspirin before I get here!" blurted out Dennis. "My head is spinning now!"

The men laughed, got up from the table, and headed out the door. After they said their good-byes, the men got into their cars and left the parking lot, heading toward home. Linden turned off the radio while he drove so he could think about the morning's conversation. Speaking out loud, he said, "If it is true that God had to do a work in my heart for me to come to Him, then He had to have had mercy on me. Why did He have mercy on me and not on my next-door neighbor, who is as lost as he can be! I am no better than him. I am a sinner just like him. But I follow Christ, and he doesn't. I am certainly not smarter than him, and the Lord knows I have witnessed to him; however, He doesn't see what I see."

At that moment, a wave of humility washed over his soul. The verses in Romans 9 began to replay in his mind over and over again as well as the verses from Ephesians that the men had just discussed: "I will have mercy on whom I will have mercy." (Romans 9: 15) "This is not of your own doing; it is a gift from God." (Ephesians 2:8) "God in His sovereignty—chose me!"

Linden quickly pulled his car to the side of the road as the tears began to cloud his vision. *Why me?* he thought. *Why me?* He put the car in park, bowed his head and wept.

Chapter Eight

CONTRADICTIONS?

"I know, Linden, it is overwhelming," replied Dennis as they discussed the previous week's conversation with Bro. John over lunch. "Just to think that the God of the universe said you are one whom I will show mercy is beyond comprehension."

"I am still sorting this out, Dennis, because I have found so many verses that speak of election in the scripture and those that seem to say that election is for everyone. I just know that I was overcome with a sense of awe at what God had done for me, an undeserving sinner. It still chokes me up," acknowledged Linden as his voice broke.

"Me, too, my friend. I guess that's why they call it 'amazing grace,' because it truly is amazing," said Dennis. "But you know, I found many scriptures that also affirm that everyone can believe. How do we know which is which, what is what, if you know what I mean?"

Linden looked a little confused by his friend's choice of words but quickly responded by asking, "What verses did you find concerning our assignment?"

"Well, to begin with," stated Dennis, "there is the old standby found in John 3:16 that says,

> "For God so loved the world that he gave His only son, that whoever believes in Him should not perish but have eternal life." (John 3:16)

That verse implies that God's love for the world includes everybody, so therefore, anyone who believes will have eternal life. I also remembered John 1:12 that says,

> "But as many as have received Him, to them He gave the right to become children of God, to those who believe in His name." (John 1:12)

My question to Bro. John would be, 'Is this saying that many could be anybody, or does it imply that 'many' is a word that has its limits, you know, like 'many' but not everybody?'"

"I think I follow you," remarked Linden. "How do we know if 'many' means everyone? I found other verses when I went to my Bible concordance, looked up the word 'many,' and I found an interesting verse in Acts 13: 48. Let me read it to you. It says,

> "And when the Gentiles heard this, they began rejoicing and glorifying the word of the Lord and as many as were appointed to eternal life believed." (Acts 13:48)

After he read the verse, Linden asserted, "I think the use of 'many' implies a limited number, according to this verse."

"I agree," surmised Dennis, "but what about those scriptures that talks about Jesus dying for the whole world? I went to my concordance also just like you taught me and looked up words like salvation, election, chosen, the world, and anything related to salvation. I found some interesting verses in 1 Timothy 2:3-5. I wrote them out on a three-by-five card so I could show them to Bro. John. It says this:

> "This is good and it is pleasing in the sight of God our Savior, who desires all people to be saved and to come to the knowledge of the truth. For there is one God and there is one mediator between God and men, the man Christ Jesus, who gave Himself a ransom for all, which is the testimony given at the proper time.' (1 Timothy 2:3-5)

"I also found something very interesting in 2 Peter. In the very first chapter, he tells those to whom he is writing to make sure of their election. So the word election is used, I guess, to prove that God does elect people, but does He elect all people or just some? I ask this question because later on in chapter three and verse nine, Peter writes these words." Dennis took another three-by-five card in his hand and read,

> "The Lord is not slow to fulfill His promise as some count slowness, but is patient toward you, not wishing that any should perish, but that all should reach repentance."
> (2 Peter 3:9)

"So what is it, Linden?" asked Dennis. "Are only some elect, or can everybody be one of the elect if they just believe? Looking at these verses, it seems that the Apostle Peter is contradicting himself."

"I have the same questions, Dennis, because I found some verses that seem to contradict themselves," inferred Linden. "For example, Matthew 11:27 says the following." Linden flipped the pages of his Bible to the book of Matthew and read,

> "All things have been handed over to me by my Father, and no one knows the Son except the Father, and no one knows the Father except the Son and anyone to whom the Son chooses to reveal him." (Matthew 11:27)

"Now if I am reading this right, Jesus seems to be saying that there is a limited number of people to whom He chooses to reveal Himself. Therefore, this supports Romans 9 in the fact that God has mercy on whom He will have mercy. It is God's choice. However, if you read the next verse it says,

> "Come to me, all who labor and are heavy laden and I will give you rest. Take my yoke upon you, and learn from me, for I am gentle and lowly in heart, and you will find rest for your souls. For my yoke is easy and my burden is light."
> (Matthew 11:28)

"So, who doesn't labor, and who isn't heavy laden? It would seem that everyone falls into this category. Therefore, anyone can come.

So does Jesus contradict Himself? He tells us in John 6, which we read with Bro. John, that no one can come to Him unless the Father draws him. Now He says, 'Come to me.' Boy, Bro. John has some explaining to do!"

"Maybe we should call him and ask him if he wants to do a sleepover so we can pick his brain all day and night because I have so many questions!" replied Dennis, rather amused at all the information they found.

"Well, Saturday should be interesting to say the least. I hope he is ready to stay for breakfast and lunch. We might be there awhile!" declared Linden.

Both men looked at their watches and agreed that they needed to get back to work. With a friendly pat on the back and a handshake, they parted company. Linden thought to himself as he walked out of the local fast-food chain where they had met, *So many questions, so little time!*

Chapter Nine

POTENTIAL OR ACTUAL?

"Great work, guys! You really did your homework," expressed Bro. John as he reviewed Dennis's three-by-five cards and the two pages of scripture references and questions given to him by Linden. "By the way, there are several folks here today who are praying for you guys as we have our conversation."

"Really?" asked Linden. "They are praying for us as we speak?"

"Well, if you look to your right at the two tables in the back of the cafe, you will see the men I am talking about," said Bro. John.

Both Linden and Dennis peered across the room only to see a few of the men staring back at them, smiling, and then waving!

"So you pre-warned them we were coming today?" asked Dennis.

"Oh, no, they know you have been meeting with me every Saturday for these last three weeks and hopefully a couple of more weeks if all goes well today," replied Bro. John. "So they have been praying for you when they see you come in, but particularly today."

"And what is so special about today?" implored Linden.

"Today we discuss a topic that some really get hung up on. It's the day we talk about for whom Christ died. From the questions you gave me this morning and looking over the scriptures that you found that speak about salvation, Christ's death and so forth, our discussion will prompt many questions in your mind concerning this doctrine of election. Some of our discussion might fly in the face of what you have been taught. It also may cause you to want to string me up! So we need prayer!" said Bro. John, somewhat jokingly but also somewhat reservedly.

Both men looked at each other rather apprehensively and then turned to the waitress as she stood beside their table, filling their cups with coffee.

"Better leave the carafe, young lady. Looks like we will need to be wide awake for this conversation," declared Linden.

The men chuckled, and Bro. John asked if he could pray over the breakfast and for them. They ate their breakfast while they enjoyed talking about the weather, a little politics, and a little football. After they ate and pushed their plates to the front of the table so the waitress could grab them easily, Bro. John once again picked up the three-by-five cards and the notes. As he did, he said, "Guys, you have many good questions, and the scriptures you brought to the table today are very good. Looking over them, I see that you found some that talk about all men being saved and that God loved the world or dies for the sins of the world. I want you to know at the very outset of the conversation that you may not agree with everything I have to say. We may not get to all the questions you have because we don't have the time to go into exhaustive explanations this morning. Also, the more I explain the reformed position, the more questions will come to your mind. I will not answer all of them because I want you to do some digging on your own. Remember, Linden, you came to me to ask about election. I was more than willing to tell you what we believe, but I will not coerce you or force you two to believe what I believe. I want you to honestly hear this position and then to decide if the scripture teaches these doctrines. If so, you are left with a choice. That choice is to believe or not believe. Agreed?" asked Bro. John.

"Agreed," said Linden.

Dennis nodded his head and said emphatically, "Agreed, good sir!"

"All right then, let me begin our conversation with this statement, and I want you to really digest it and then respond to it," commenced Bro. John. "If Jesus died for the whole world, then the whole world is saved. Let's go home!"

Bro. John did not say another word but instead cut his pancakes with his fork, put a large chunk in his mouth, and began to chew. He slowly looked up to see a somewhat startled look in both men's faces, which caused him to smile.

"Well, any responses?" asked the pastor.

Both men looked at each other as if to say, "You first." Linden shrugged his shoulders timidly and said, "I'll give it a go."

Dennis let out a sigh of relief while he stated, "Man, I am so glad you're going first. I don't know what to say!"

"Me neither, but here goes," replied Linden. "Pastor, not everyone is saved in the world, so how can you say that everyone is saved?" inquired Linden.

"Think about the question again, Linden. If Jesus died for the whole world and by his death paid the penalty for our sins, then everything is paid in full. No more worries. Mission accomplished," countered Bro. John. "Think back to our early conversations and examine this statement in light of those discussions."

Linden quickly reviewed in his mind the conversations that they had previously had. He knew they had talked about God's sovereignty, about man's condition of not seeking God, of the will being affected by the fall, of God having mercy on whom He would have mercy, but this was stumping him. *If Jesus died for all, then all would be saved,* he thought. *What is it that I am not getting?* After he reflected for a moment, he finally spoke to Bro. John and said, "I'm stumped. Perhaps my mind is not working today, but I'm not getting what you are getting at, if that makes sense, Bro. John."

"Let me see if I can jog your brain a little bit, Linden," said Bro. John. "If you remember from our first conversation, we concluded that God is sovereign over all and what He purposes, He accomplishes. Now I want you to hear a couple of scriptures that might help you with the statement I made."

Bro. John opened his Bible and turned to Acts 2:23. He read,

> "This Jesus, delivered up according to the definite plan and foreknowledge of God, you crucified and killed by the hands of lawless men." (Acts 2:23)

After he finished reading this passage, he quickly turned to Matthew 1:21 and read,

> "She will bear a son and you shall call his name Jesus, for He will save his people from their sins." (Matthew 1:21)

Bro. John looked up from his Bible and asked, "If God determined that Jesus would die and it was prophesied by the angel to Joseph that Jesus would save his people from their sins, does not God accomplish all He has determined?"

Linden gazed across the table at Bro. John and said, "So, if I am thinking correctly, you are saying that if Jesus died for everyone, then because God had determined it to be so and He came to die for sins, then Jesus accomplished what He came to do according to God's plan. Am I thinking correctly?" asked Linden.

"You are on the right track. Now think it through and keep going," said Bro. John.

"Okay," responded Linden. "Let's see . . . Jesus died for sins, and He died for the sins of everyone. Then logically, if He accomplished God's will in dying for those sins, then sins are forgiven, and the debt has been paid for everyone. But not all believe in Jesus, so I would have to conclude that Jesus did not pay for their sins."

Dennis now sat up straight in his chair and replied to Linden's words. "Wait a minute, Linden," said Dennis. "God accomplishes all He sets out to accomplish. If Jesus died for the sins of the world, then we have to conclude that the world will be saved or God's plan and will is not accomplished."

"Excellent!" shouted Bro. John. "Both of you are beginning to see the problem if we say that Jesus died for the whole world, meaning everyone in the world."

"But I am still not totally clear about the implications of your statement, Bro. John," declared Linden.

"Let me explain it this way, Linden," voiced Bro. John. "Let's say that Jesus died for the sins of the world. On the cross, Jesus said, 'It is finished.' His death finished the sacrifice for sins, and the penalty was paid. He bore the punishment for our sins. If He bore the punishment for the whole world, then God would not punish anyone because Jesus bore the punishment. Everyone has now had their sins paid for, so we have no more worries about who gets to heaven if you believe that Jesus died for everyone. Yet, as you stated, not everyone believes in Jesus. So, how can unbelievers have their sins paid for, if Jesus paid for everyone's sin, yet not believe in Jesus as their Savior? Are their sins paid for or not? Or are they potentially paid for until a person believes? Now think that through before you answer," requested Bro. John.

Linden spoke up and said, "It would seem that it is a potential payment until someone believes, but you are probably going to tell me that I am incorrect, correct?"

Bro. John laughed and then said, "Let's follow that it is potential. What makes it actually apply to the person? It would have to be his faith in what Christ did on the cross. Yet since it is only a potential payment until a person believes, then who holds the key to eternal life? Man does, not God! In other words, God's will is thwarted by His creatures' will to accept or reject the offer of salvation. Remember, in one of our first meetings, that we discussed the sovereignty of God?"

Linden responded, "Yes, according to scripture, God does as He pleases, and no one can withstand His hand or His purpose."

As quickly as the statement was spoken, a light went off in Linden's mind. He slapped his forehead with his hand and barked, "Now I get it! If Christ's salvation was only potential, then God can will whatever He wants to in the universe except when it comes to man. He then leaves that decision to man. But how can man make a decision for Christ if he is dead in his trespasses and sins?"

"Now you are putting it together, Linden," affirmed Bro. John. "If you follow the 'potential' route, you find that man becomes sovereign over salvation, not God. You also have to conclude that Christ's death does not actually save anyone. It only has the potential to save. Yet we just read that Jesus came to save His people from their sins. Notice that it said 'His' people and not 'everyone.' The word 'His' speaks to the extent of His sacrifice. Those who hold to the reformed view believe it is limited to those who have been chosen by God before we were ever created. Now, Linden, you said that there are those who do not believe in Jesus. If we continue to follow the non-reformist belief that Jesus died for everyone, then salvation never is applied to many, many millions who are lost. Not only does Jesus bear the punishment for their sins, if He died for everyone, they are still being punished for their sins. According to the non-reformist view, there will be a double punishment—one for Jesus and one for them."

Dennis chimed in quickly, "So, you are saying that when Jesus died for the sins of His people, he actually saved them?"

"That is exactly what I am saying, Dennis," responded Bro. John. "That is why I said that if Jesus died for everyone and if God's will is not thwarted by anything or anyone, then God actually saves everyone by the death of His Son. But we know that not everyone believes. So, we must conclude that Jesus died for a specific people, His chosen people, and that His death actually saves them, not potentially saves them. We call this 'particular redemption', in that God, from before the foundation of the world, chose or elected individuals from the human race to be the objects of His grace and mercy. How many did He choose, we don't know. But I believe it to be millions and millions of people throughout the ages of time. And when He chose them, in His time, He called them to Himself so they could be saved, and He continually calls His chosen today. He actually saves His elect."

"But what about all those passages we found that talk about God loving the world and dying for the sins of the world?" asked Linden.

"Okay," said Bro. John, "let's talk about that for a minute. But first, did you see the news report about the turmoil in the Middle East over the developing nuclear capabilities of certain countries?" asked Bro. John.

Both men looked at each other quickly and then back at the pastor. "What's that got to do with anything, Bro. John?" inquired Dennis.

"Just thought I would take a quick break from such a heavy discussion," said Bro. John. "Everybody is certainly watching them, aren't they?" he asked. "I mean, all the world has their eye on the Middle East."

"I know it has everybody's attention here in the States," remarked Dennis.

"We're all worried that nuclear weapons will fall into the hands of some tyrant that doesn't need it," declared Linden.

Bro. John sat back in his chair and smiled while he prepared to take another sip of his coffee. "Before I take another swig of this coffee that everybody loves, do you understand what you just said?" he asked.

"Yeah," said Dennis, "we're concerned about the Middle East."

"But is everybody paying attention to the Middle East?" petitioned Bro. John to both men. "Is all the world paying attention, and by the term 'world,' do I mean that individuals, individuals in every nation, or just leaders in those nations are paying attention? Is everyone in Africa concerned? Boys, girls, men, and women? What about the animals? Are they concerned?" he continued to ask.

"What are you getting at, pastor? asked Linden.

"I want you to see that the terms we use when we mention the words 'all' and 'everybody' and even the term 'world' has various meanings," explained Bro. John. "It is the same in scripture. You have to let the context speak when using those words as well as letting any implications in scripture be subservient to that which is explicitly taught. Let me give you a couple of examples. Turn in your Bibles to the Gospel of Luke 2:1."

As Bro. John saw that they had found the reference, he read,

> *"In those days a decree went out from Caesar Augustus that all the world should be registered." (Luke 2:1)*

"Now tell me, men, did everyone in the whole world go to be registered?" asked Bro. John.

"Well, everyone who was ruled by the Romans had to register," said Linden.

"Very good," responded Bro. John. "But not everyone in the whole world had to be registered because those who dwelt in China were not under Roman rule. So we must conclude that the term 'all' does not really mean everyone in this context and the term 'world' is limited to a certain geographical location where Roman rule existed. Now let me take you to the verse that non-reformist hang their hat on to prove that Christ died for everyone. You know it by heart. It's John 3:16."

Bro. John recited,

> *"For God so loved the world that He gave his only Son, that whoever believes in Him should not perish but have eternal life." (John 3:16)*

"Now we discussed Jesus' teaching concerning the ability of man and concluded that man does not have the moral ability to choose Christ, right?" asked Bro. John.

"Yes, that is what I believe it is saying," said Linden. Dennis nodded his head in the affirmative as well.

"In spite of that, non-reformist argue that John 3:16 is evidence that man still has some ability to choose Christ because of the use of the word 'world' and 'whoever.' Tell me ... does this verse say anything about man's ability to choose Christ?" inquired Bro. John.

"Not that I can see," replied Linden.

"Dennis, tell me what the verse says please—" asked Bro. John.

"All I can see it saying is that whoever believes will inherit eternal life," stated Dennis.

"Even though God loves the world, does it say that man now has the ability to choose Christ, just because God is a loving God?" asked Bro. John.

"Okay, I think I understand where you're going," said Linden. "We cannot assume that God has given everyone the ability to choose based on one verse but must take the total teaching of the scripture on the subject of election and all its components."

"That is right, Linden," replied Bro. John. "All this verse says is that whoever believes will have eternal life. The reformed believer will tell you that those who believe are the ones whom God gave to Jesus to grant eternal life based on the teachings of Jesus, Paul, and the other writers of scripture. You could also say of the term 'world' that God has a general love for mankind or the world but a specific love for His elect who are in that world."

"Okay, you lost me on that one, pastor!" declared Dennis.

Bro. John laughed and then explained, "These doctrines are so wonderful but also take time to study and reflect on, and it can't all be explained over a few breakfast meetings. Let me see if I can explain it to you this way. Let's say you have a son and I have a son. I meet your son, and I really like him and develop a relationship with him. As a pastor, I could say that I have come to love and respect your son. However, if you came to me and asked me to pay for his college, clothe him, and feed him, I would have to decline. I have a general love for your son, but the person I am going to send to college, clothe, and feed is my own son. Why? Because I have a specific love for him that I don't have for your son. Now that might be a way to explain the general love of God and the specific love of God. He has chosen His elect and loves them with a love that actually saves them because He loved them so much that He sent His son for them, to die for them and to pay the penalty of their sins in full. Now that is a lot to grasp, but I want you guys to really ponder and meditate over the scriptures you gave me and see if the terms used in those verses can only be defined in one sense only. Or are there different meanings depending on the context in which it is used and in accord with the explicit teachings of the scripture concerning election?"

Sensing that Bro. John was about to wrap up their meeting for the day, Linden quickly asked, "Bro. John, before we go, could you explain to me 2 Peter 3:9 because my wife asked how the doctrine of election squares with the fact that Peter says God wants everyone to reach repentance."

"Okay, turn to that passage, and as you do, I will read it to you," said Bro. John. He read,

> *"The Lord is not slow to fulfill His promise as some count slowness, but is patient towards you, not wishing that any should perish but that all should reach repentance."* (2 Peter 3:9)

"First, let's see to whom Peter is writing. Dennis, look at the beginning of chapter three verse one and tell me what you discern from the first part of that verse," said Bro. John.

Dennis read,

> *"This is now the second letter that I am writing to you, beloved."* (2 Peter 3:1)

"I guess he is saying that there was another letter that was first, so would that be 1 Peter?" asked Dennis.

"I believe you are right," proclaimed Bro. John. "Now turn to 1 Peter and read the first two verses."

Dennis flipped back toward 1 Peter, and when he found the reference, he read the following:

> *"Peter, an apostle of Jesus Christ, to those who are elect exiles of the dispersion in Pontus, Galatia, Cappadocia, Asia, and Bithynia, according to the foreknowledge of God the Father, in the sanctification of the Spirit, for obedience to Jesus Christ and for sprinkling with his blood: may grace and peace be multiplied to you."* (1 Peter 1:1-2)

"So, guys, let me ask you some questions," stated Bro. John. "Who were the recipients of this letter?" he asked.

"Chapter one says it was to the elect in these places," said Linden.

"So can we then believe that Peter is still writing to these same people based on chapter three of 2 Peter?" queried Bro. John.

"I believe that can be deduced from these verses," stated Dennis.

"Okay, now if you believe that Peter is writing to the elect, then as you read verse nine of chapter three, be sure to see that when Peter says God is patient, who is God patient toward?" asked Bro. John.

Linden and Dennis both looked again at the passage, and Linden spoke, "Peter uses the words 'toward you' in the verse."

"Very good, Linden," responded Bro. John. "Now if you interpret the verse, making sure you do not skip over the words 'toward you' like many people do, then you see that this verse could mean that there are those of the elect that have not yet reached repentance. Could you see it that way?" asked Bro. John.

"I see the bigger context also, pastor," stated Linden. "The whole context of chapter three is talking about Christ's return, so Peter is talking about those who have not come to repentance yet before His return, but he is specifically talking to those to whom he is writing. So it doesn't have anything to do with atonement or a proof that God wants everyone to be saved!" exclaimed Linden.

"Now do you see why you need to keep everything in context, read the scripture in light of its explicit teachings, and make sure you don't leave out words like some do to garner a proof text to support their point?" asked Bro. John.

"Wow!" asserted Linden. "Wait until I explain this to the wife! I can't tell you how many times I used that verse myself to prove that God wants everyone to be saved."

"I know," said Bro. John. "We have all been guilty of that. Hey, listen, men. I have to be running, but next week, I have something for you that will be totally irresistible."

"Well," inquired Dennis, "can you give us a hint?"

"Patience once again, my friends. But remember, I have not gone through all your verses that you came up with, but I am trusting that you will dig deeper into them and apply what we have been speaking of today. I want these conversations to drive you into the teachings of the scripture so you can come to an understanding of these doctrines on your own. Then you can make a decision based on your study as to whether or not you will embrace them. Gotta go. See you next week!" shouted Bro. John as he moved quickly toward the door and waved to his members who were dining at the other tables.

"You know, Dennis," said Linden as they got up from the table, "some of this is really making sense to me. How about you?" he asked.

"I'm still mulling it over in my mind, but the more I study, the more inclined I am to believe it," stated Dennis.

"See you Tuesday?" asked Linden.

"Yes, I will be there," said Dennis. "Are you bringing up this topic?"

"I told our group that I would report what we are learning, so I guess it will be our topic for the morning's Bible study," replied Linden.

"In that case, I think I'll sleep in!" joked Dennis.

"If you are not there, I will personally come get you! I have a feeling I will need backup!" expressed Linden.

The men shook hands and got into their cars. As Linden started the engine, he sent up a prayer to the Lord: "Lord, Tuesday's coming! Help me explain what needs explaining!"

Chapter Ten

ABSOLUTE HERESY!

"There is no way I'm going to believe that!" voiced Henry. "To say that Jesus didn't die for everyone is absolute heresy, and we shouldn't even discuss it anymore."

"Linden, you know our church doesn't believe what you are saying. It is not within our doctrinal statement. We believe that all have the chance to hear the gospel and all have an opportunity to respond by either accepting or rejecting Christ." retorted Joe as he pushed his plate away from him.

"Please listen to what I am saying, men," pleaded Linden. "Ever since we came upon the word election in our study, I have been researching, reading, and discussing what it means for the last four weeks. It is my understanding that those who adhere to the doctrine of election are not saying they run out and find who are the elect and witness to them only. They present the gospel to all, knowing that those who respond do so because God has enabled them to come to Him."

"So, are you saying they continue to present the gospel to everyone?" asked Alvin. "If they are doing what we do already, then what's the big deal?" he concluded.

"Well," chimed in Dennis, "it is my understanding that it comes down to who is sovereign in salvation, man or God."

Linden added, "I'm not saying that I understand everything about election or Calvinism, as it is called, but what Bro. John has taught us makes sense. And it aligns more with scripture than what I have been taught. So, at this point, I am more inclined to believe in the doctrine of election than I previously was."

"You need to quit listening to that man, Linden," interjected Henry. "Calvinism is divisive, and as I said, to say that Jesus didn't die for everyone is heresy!"

"Henry, calling people heretics is a very serious charge," declared Linden. "When you say someone is a heretic, you are saying they are unorthodox in their beliefs and that those whom you call heretics are in denial of revealed truths as well as believing what is in error. When you say something like that, you have lumped together some of the greatest Christian theologians that have ever lived, men who have come to the same conclusions through their study of scripture as Bro. John has explained to me. I know this because I went to the Internet to find Christians in the past who held to these doctrines and their numbers are overwhelming. So, please be careful in what you say concerning heresy and heretics. But as we talked about Saturday, if Jesus died for the sins of the whole world, then the whole world would be saved. That is the logical conclusion since God accomplishes His purposes in salvation."

"I just don't see the fairness in what you are saying, Linden," said Henry. "Everyone needs to have the chance to accept or reject the gospel."

"Bro. John told us that many people get stuck on the point of fairness," stated Dennis, "but what we just read in Romans 9 tells us that God has mercy on whom He will have mercy. Bro. John also asked us if we think God is obligated to save anyone. When you think about it, Henry, God is not obligated to save anyone. That He chose to save whom He wants to save is nothing more than grace and mercy on His part. He didn't have to do that!"

There was an awkward silence that fell across the table after Dennis finished speaking. Joe finally spoke and said, "Linden, Dennis, if you guys are leaning toward this teaching, does this mean that our Bible study time going to continue along this line?"

"No, Joe, we are going on in our study of Romans. But we agreed to learn about the doctrine of election, and all of us agreed to do so," said Linden. "I do want everyone to be objective and not combative about this issue. We can agree to disagree, should any of us decide one way or the other about election. We must walk in love in our attitudes. Whatever you conclude, everyone has to have some working belief about election. It is not something we can skip over or discount because we don't like it or don't know anything about it. But understand that my conversations with Bro. John have not concluded. He said we were going to talk about something irresistible this coming Saturday. So I need to know if you want to hear of that conversation at our next meeting before we move forward. Is everyone game?" he asked.

"As long as it is an overview and that we move forward," suggested Joe.

All the men agreed and decided to hear the findings of Linden and Dennis at their next meeting. Linden closed with a prayer. The men shook hands and left the cafe for work. As Linden approached his car, he heard steps behind him, turned, and found Juan and Paul following him. As they came by the side of Linden's car, Juan said, "Linden, Paul and I are probably the oldest ones in this group. We have been through many studies, and we heard about the doctrine of election from another Bible group leader years ago. We know it can be divisive if people let it. Paul and I discussed what we learned back then, and we have been leaning toward this teaching for many years. We just haven't said anything. I guess you could call us 'closet Calvinists.'"

The men smiled, and Linden responded, "I never knew you guys held these beliefs."

Paul said, "Linden, we know that you cannot escape the word 'election' in the scripture. It's there, and at some point in your life, if you are going to be serious about Bible study, you have to look at all the sides of this issue. Like you, we were taught something different. But from our last study and now this one, these teachings have more scriptural support than any other view we held. We don't know all there is to know, but we would like to learn more."

"That's why we wanted to speak with you away from the group," said Juan. "We have a question to ask."

"Okay, go ahead. Ask away," responded Linden.

"Do you mind if Paul and I meet with you, Dennis, and the pastor this Saturday?" Juan asked.

"Well, the pastor did say the more, the merrier, so I don't think he would mind at all! So I will see you Saturday at 7:00 a.m.," replied Linden. "Hey, now that I think about it, you know what will make it even merrier?" he asked.

Both men were a little puzzled but inquisitive, and Juan asked, "No, what will make it merrier? More people?"

"No," said Linden. "It will be merrier if you buy my breakfast!"

Linden winked, bid the men farewell, opened his door, and slid into the front seat. *This should be interesting*, he thought. *Very interesting.*

Chapter Eleven

NEW RECRUITS

Bro. John's facial expression was priceless as he saw Linden walking into the Town Cafe with not only Dennis but two other men in tow. Linden smiled as he approached the table where Bro. John was seated and promptly said, "Pastor, I think we need a bigger table!"

"Are you out recruiting, Linden?" asked Bro. John as he rose to shake the hands of his new guests.

"Pastor, these are two of our friends from our Bible study. This is Juan, and this is Paul," answered Linden. "They asked if they could join us, especially when I told them that we were going to talk about something irresistible. They said they couldn't resist!"

Bro. John greeted the men, asked the waitress if she could seat them at a larger table, and spoke with both men about their families and asked a few questions about their background while she waited. Once seated at a larger table and the coffee served, Bro. John asked both Paul and Juan why they came.

"I'll start," said Juan. "We wanted to continue to learn about the doctrines you have been talking with Linden and Dennis. We were exposed to them a few years ago by a Bible study leader and embraced their teachings."

Paul quickly added, "Our Bible study leader moved, and we didn't really dive into a deeper study but discussed these teachings among ourselves over the last couple of years. We have been keeping our beliefs to ourselves. We were excited to hear what you've been sharing with Linden and Dennis, and we decided it was time for us to step up to the plate and declare that we are reformed in our beliefs and offer our support to them."

"Great!" exclaimed Bro. John. "Now you know that I am not trying to coerce Linden and Dennis in any way to become Calvinists. In fact, I have been presenting to them the basic beliefs of the reformed faith and allowing them to form their own opinions. They have been great students, and they are digging deeper into the scriptures to see if what I say is valid and according to biblical teachings. I'm glad you could join us today."

After more small talk while they were waiting for their waitress to return to take their orders, Bro. John decided to introduce his topic for the day. He looked at the men and said, "Guys, a long time ago, there was a certain man who was walking to a certain city to persecute Christians. While walking along, minding his own business, a light from heaven flashed all around him, and he fell to the ground. He also heard a voice speaking to him and discovered that the voice came from Jesus. You probably recognize from this story that I am talking about the Apostle Paul or Saul, as he was named, before his encounter with Jesus. From this encounter, we know that Jesus told Ananias to go to Saul while he was blind and to lay his hands on him so he could see. He also told Ananias that Saul was his chosen instrument to go to preach to the Gentiles. Now, once Jesus revealed Himself to Saul, could he have resisted Jesus' call on his life?" he asked.

The men thought about Bro. John's question for a few moments, and then Dennis spoke up, "In light of what we have learned, if Paul was God's chosen instrument, then God accomplishes what He has purposed. Therefore, I would have to say that Paul could not have resisted this call on his life."

"You are right, Dennis. Congratulations," cheered Bro. John. "But did you know the non-reformed do not believe that? Their belief is that the Holy Spirit gave enough grace to Paul and any others whom the Lord calls to make the decision themselves, but they still have the opportunity to reject His call."

"But wait a minute," chimed in Juan. "God chose Paul. If Paul was chosen by God, how can Paul un-choose himself?"

"Good question, Juan," replied Bro. John. "If Paul could un-choose himself, then God's calling does not really have any effectiveness to it at all. God would be very unsatisfied and disappointed with Himself that He could not accomplish what He set out to accomplish, namely the choosing and calling of Paul because Paul could reject it."

"So, it goes back to God accomplishing what He set out to accomplish, mainly that He chose the elect. Therefore, He will bring the elect to salvation, right?" asked Linden.

"That's right," agreed Bro. John. "If you have your Bibles, which you do, turn to Romans 8:30."

When the men had found the passage, Bro. John read,

> "And those whom He predestined He also called, and those He called he also justified, and those He justified he also glorified." (Romans 8:30)

"Men," said Bro. John, "when God predestined those or chose those whom He would grant salvation, He also called them. The call they received was not just an outward call. It was an inward call by the Holy Spirit of God that made them alive so they could respond in faith. If you look at the progression of this verse, those He called are also justified or made right in the sight of God. We know that justification occurs when a person places their faith in Christ. Now that faith is given as a gift from God. The only way a person can have faith is if they have been quickened or made alive as we discussed last week. If a person has been made alive, then they will respond in faith because now they have a new nature, one that desires to follow Christ. If that desire is in their hearts, then they will come to Christ. In fact, turn back to the Gospel of John and look for chapter six verse thirty-seven. Paul, once you find the verse, will you read it for us?" asked Bro. John.

Paul quickly found the verse and read,

> "All that the Father gives will come to me and whoever comes to me I will never cast out." (John 6:37)

"Notice in this verse, it says that whomever the Father gives to Jesus will come to Him. We call this process 'effectual calling.' All that means is that it accomplishes its desired goal. They will come! If man can resist the inward call of the spirit of God, then God's word concerning those whom He gives to Jesus, namely that they will come to Him, is false."

As soon as Bro. John finished his sentence, Linden quickly spoke and said, "You spoke of an inward call, and I heard you say something about an outward call. Can you explain what you mean?" asked Linden.

"Sure thing," replied Bro. John. "The outward call is the preaching of the gospel. It is preached to everyone, whether they are chosen or not, for we do not know who is chosen until they respond in faith because a change has been wrought in their heart. So we preach to whoever will hear. Concerning those who do not believe when they hear the gospel message, we can say that the outward call did not 'effect' salvation because they did not believe. Therefore, the outward call can be resisted because the unregenerate person does not desire or want Christ in the first place. In fact, they want to run from Christ. When the gospel is preached to those who are chosen, the Holy Spirit issues an inward call to the elect, and they believe because the call will result in them coming to Christ. Did that answer your question?" inquired Bro. John.

"Yes, it did," responded Linden.

"Good. Now let me ask you a question. If a person has been made new or made alive from being in the state of spiritual death, will they want to resist the inward call of the spirit?"

Linden thought for a moment and then answered, "If their will was affected in the fall of man, then they were not willing to come in the first place. They did not want to come because they had no desire to come. Now they have been made willing or have a desire for Christ because the spirit of God has wrought a change in them. You told us that we make our choices according to our strongest inclinations or desire. So, if my thinking is straight, if they desire Christ, they will not resist what they want to do, and that is to embrace Christ by faith. Correct?" asked Linden.

"Class dismissed!" proclaimed Bro. John. "My work is done. You are right, Linden!" The men laughed, but Bro. John continued, "In all seriousness, that is why it is called 'irresistible grace' because their hearts have been changed or regenerated. Their wills have been made willing, if you please, and God draws them to Himself. Nothing can thwart His will, and since it is His will that they come, they will not resist because they do not want to resist."

"Bro. John," said Juan, "if the elect are going to come to Christ, then why do we witness?"

"Another good question, Juan," replied the pastor. "Your question has been an objection given by those who are not reformed since before the days of Calvin! Let's answer that from scripture. Turn in your Bibles to Romans 10 and look at verse fourteen and following."

The men found the passage, and Bro. John read the following:

> *"How then will they call on Him in whom they have not believed? And how are they to believe in Him of whom they have never heard? And how are they to hear without someone preaching? And how are they to preach unless they are sent? As it is written, "How beautiful are the feet of those who preach the good news!" But they have not all obeyed the gospel. For Isaiah says, "Lord, who has believed what he has heard from us?" So faith comes by hearing and hearing through the word of Christ."*
> *(Romans 10:14-17)*

After he read the passage, Bro. John explained, "Men, Paul is telling the recipients of the Book of Romans that a person cannot believe in Jesus unless someone tells them about Him. How can a person believe in an invention if the invention has not been made? It would be impossible. So, Paul is saying that a person must hear the gospel to be able to believe the gospel. In the reformed belief, we believe that God has not only ordained the ends but also the means whereby a person is saved. A person must hear the gospel, whether through preaching, witnessing, reading the scripture, or whatever means a person employs to tell others about Christ. The Holy Spirit is the one who quickens the heart. This is done in secret. We do not know who He is calling and regenerating. We must present the gospel to everyone. That is why we give the general call because we do not know who the elect are. The specific call is in God's hands."

Dennis quickly asked, "So, it is not true that reformed believers don't do evangelism?"

"No, it is not true that we do not witness. Not only do we witness, but the doctrine of election encourages evangelism," said Bro. John.

"How so?" inquired Linden.

"Well," said Bro. John, "if you know that God has elected people unto salvation and you know they will come to Him because His calling will accomplish what He desires, then you have great confidence knowing that as you witness and preach, the elect will respond. But remember, God has ordained the means by which they come, and that is witnessing, preaching and proclaiming the gospel. So, as long as you are doing those things, someone will respond. We still have the responsibility to proclaim and proclaim the good news we must."

"Along those lines, pastor," remarked Paul, "Juan and I discovered in our study and conversations over the last couple of years that many of the men God used to flame revival over America and other parts of the world during the eighteenth and nineteenth centuries held these doctrines to be scriptural and preached them as such."

"You're right, Juan," replied Bro. John. "Names such as Jonathan Edwards, George Whitefield, Charles Spurgeon and William Carey, who founded one of the very first missionary societies and has been called the father of modern missions, all of these men held to the doctrine of divine election. They knew that God had ordained the means of preaching and witnessing to call His elect. They fulfilled that calling faithfully, and God used them mightily."

"Why is it then that those who hold to the reformed doctrines are accused of not being evangelistic?" asked Dennis.

"Sadly," responded Bro. John, "many who do hold that opinion jump to the false conclusion that since God knows His elect, He will get them to come to Him as if He waves a magic wand and *poof*, they come. They do not take into consideration that He has ordained the means by which they come, and that is the proclaiming of the gospel. Others hold that opinion because there are some in the reformed camp who have moved far to the right of the reformers and developed a system called "Hyper-Calvinism," which has stated that God doesn't need our help to bring His elect to Himself. I believe both these positions are wrong and that the objection that we are not evangelistic must be dealt with in a scriptural manner and a loving manner. One thing I want to remind you of, men, is that you are not called to go around starting arguments about the reformed faith. We are called to defend the faith, but when we do so, it must be in love. You are also called to proclaim the gospel to everyone in love."

Bro. John pushed his plate aside, topped of his coffee cup with some hot coffee from the carafe sitting on the table, and continued, "Men, over the last three or four weeks, I have given you the basic tenets of the reformed faith. I have purposely not delved into every issue or answered every question yet hopefully have stimulated your mind so that you would dive deeper into the scripture to see if these things are true. If you can persevere and meet me again next week at this same time, I would like to give you a list of some scriptural references to study along with a list of some books that you might like to read to further your study. I do hope you can persevere one last time," stated Bro. John.

"I know that I can be here and the other men as well," Linden said as he looked toward the other men at the table. They all affirmed that they would be in attendance, and Linden quickly added, "Please pray for us as I discuss what we discussed today at our Bible study on Tuesday. Not everyone at our Bible study is receptive to this teaching."

"Why don't we end our time together in prayer? I will lead us, so let's pray," said Bro. John.

After Bro. John concluded his prayer, the men moved from the table to the parking lot where they said their good-byes. Dennis, who rode with Linden to the breakfast meeting, looked over at Linden while he was driving out of the parking lot and said, "You know, Linden, these past few weeks have been so helpful. It was really a sovereign act of God to bring me to salvation. As I look back on that time before I trusted Christ as my savior, I had heard the gospel when I was a little boy at the church where my parents took me. I even raised my hand during an invitation at Vacation Bible School and was baptized, but I lived the rest of my life as if nothing had changed. I just knew I had prayed a prayer asking Jesus into my heart, so I had my ticket to heaven and it didn't matter how I lived. But when a co-worker at the plant where I work asked me if I had any interest in spiritual things, I had to be honest, so I said no."

Linden's interest was really piqued at this moment, for he had not heard Dennis's testimony in complete detail.

"What happened next, Dennis?" asked Linden.

"I told him of my experience as a child, and he asked the question if I had changed from that moment. Again, I had to be honest with him and tell him no. My co-worker then asked if I considered myself a good person. I responded that I was. Then he asked if he could see if my goodness compared to God's standards for goodness. So, he started quoting the Ten Commandments to me and asking if I had broken any of them."

"Wow, that's an interesting way to get into the presentation of the gospel," replied Linden.

"But here's the best part, Linden," remarked Dennis. "When I began to answer him that I failed on every one, a sense of conviction came over me. I can't explain what happened, but I knew at that moment that something was missing. My co-worker went on to explain that I was separated from God because of my sin. I thought I was okay, but really, I had deceived myself all those years, thinking I had my ticket to heaven. As he explained further that Jesus came to pay the penalty for my sins that I deserved, I was overwhelmed with the grace and mercy of God. It was exactly like Bro. John has been teaching us. God opened my heart to believe in Him, and I did! It wasn't something I did or said but God who worked conviction in me first and drew me to Christ. I see so clearly that He was not obligated to do so, but out of mercy and His divine plan, he drew me to Himself that very day at work. It was all in God's timing, all in God's plan. Glory to God!"

Linden smiled and replied, "Yes, all glory to God, indeed!"

Chapter Twelve

THE WATCH

"How did the Bible study go last Tuesday?" inquired Bro. John as the men settled in their seats at the Town Cafe.

"Interesting to say the least," said Linden.

"Yeah," responded Juan. "There were those who are still adamant that we all have free will and that we can respond to God because He helps us to respond by the working of the Holy Spirit but that we have to cooperate with God to make salvation effective."

"There was also one who kept asking the question: Why does this matter?" added Paul.

"That is a legitimate question," said Bro. John. "Why does it matter?" he asked.

Linden took the lead and said, "Well, we were thrown off guard by the question because as we explained the 'general call' and the 'specific call,' our friend asked that if we were both preaching the gospel and people were responding, then what did it matter what one believed about election. We weren't sure how to answer and sound intelligent in our response."

Bro. John smiled and said, "We'll take up that topic this morning before I give you the list of scriptures I promised last week and the references so you can sound intelligent."

"Good," said Dennis. "My friends need some intelligence!"

After everyone ribbed each other about their IQs and had a good laugh or two, Bro. John proceeded with the conversation. "Before we get to that topic of why it matters, may I show you men something?" asked Bro. John.

Linden spoke up and said, "Of course, pastor, what do you have?"

Bro. John reached into his pocket and pulled out an old gold pocket watch and set it on the table. He carefully opened it, and on the inside cover of the watch was a picture of a couple that had to be taken in the early 1900s.

"Well, what do you think?" asked Bro. John.

The men each looked at the picture and guessed that it was something that had been handed down to the pastor from a family member. Before they could respond, Bro. John began the story of the watch.

"Men, I use to watch my grandfather working his garden when I was a boy. Every once in a while, he would stop and look up to see where the sun was in the sky, and then he would pull out this pocket watch from his pocket to look at the time. He would tell me that when he was growing up, he didn't have the luxury of owning a watch, so he would see where the sun was in the sky to determine what time of day it might be. When he could afford one, he told me he would still look at the sun in the sky first to see if he could determine the nearest hour and then check his watch to see how close he was in his calculations. Much of the time, he was pretty accurate. I always admired that watch. He placed this picture of him and my grandmother in it when he first bought it. He once asked me when I was in high school if I would like to have something of his when he passed from this life, and I said I would like to have his watch if no one else wanted it. To my surprise, after his death many years later, my father asked me one day to hold out my hand. In it, he placed this watch. He told me that my grandfather reminded him about two weeks before he passed away to give it to me as my inheritance from him. To this day, I treasure this watch. I keep it in a safety deposit box at my bank so I can pass it along to my children when I die."

After a moment of silence, Dennis spoke up and asked, "Is there something that you want us to know about this watch, pastor, because it seems a bit strange that you would stop our conversation about election to talk about your watch."

"You know me too well, Dennis, and only after a few weeks!" replied Bro. John. "Yes, there is something I want you to know but not so much about the watch in particular but what I do with the watch. I protect it, and I preserve it by keeping it in a safe place."

"Okay, and your point?" asked Juan, somewhat confused.

"Remember last week when I asked you if you could persevere one more week with me?" asked Bro. John.

"I remember those words exactly," said Paul. "That word is not used too much in conversations, so when you said it, I took a mental note of it and was going to ask if you thought we were not interested in hearing what you had to say. Therefore, you would want us to 'persevere' through one more week of discussion."

"I'm glad you picked up on it, but I did not believe you were bored with what I had taught you, Paul. Instead, I wanted to see if someone might pick up on the word persevere as one of the teachings of the doctrines we have been discussing," said Bro. John.

"Persevere is a doctrine?" asked Dennis as he scratched his head. "What's that got to do with the story about the watch?"

Bro. John smiled and said, "Dennis, actually, the doctrine is called 'perseverance of the saints,' which basically means that through all of life's struggles, hardship, sin, and any other thing life can throw at you, true believers will persevere until the end of their days and will not lose their salvation. Yet there is a reason that believers will persevere, and that's where the watch comes in. You see, the reason the watch is still around is because my grandfather preserved it for me and now I am preserving it for my children. I keep it safe for them. In the same way, God preserves us as His children. If you guys were turn to 1 Peter 1 and look at verses three through five for me, I would appreciate it."

The men put their Bibles in front of them and quickly turned to the passage. As Bro. John observed that they had found the passage, he began to read the following:

> "Blessed be the God and Father of our Lord Jesus Christ! According to His great mercy, he has caused us to be born again to a living hope through the resurrection of Jesus Christ from the dead, to an inheritance that is imperishable, undefiled, and unfading, kept in heaven for you, who by God's power are being guarded through faith for a salvation ready to be revealed in the last time."
> (1 Peter 1:3-5)

"Okay, men, it's question time," stated Bro. John. "Who caused us to be born again to a living hope?" Bro. John asked.

"Jesus Christ did," responded Juan.

"Correct!" Bro. John exclaimed. "Yet the verse goes on to say that we have been born again 'to' something. What was that?" he asked.

Linden replied, "To an inheritance."

"That's right, but the verse describes to us the characteristics of the inheritance. What are those characteristics, Linden?" inquired Bro. John.

Linden looked over the verse and said, "It is an inheritance that is imperishable, undefiled, unfading, and kept."

"Excellent!" Bro. John stated enthusiastically. "So, if it is imperishable, then it cannot perish. Am I right or wrong?"

Juan spoke up and said, "You are right, pastor, because the scripture says exactly that."

"Good response, Juan," declared Bro. John. "The scripture is the authority that we use to determine if a person can lose their salvation. And the scripture tells us that if it is imperishable, it will not perish, that if it is undefiled, it cannot be defiled, and that if it is unfading, it cannot fade away. However, the key to the doctrine of the perseverance of the saints is found, I believe, in the next word. It is the word 'kept.' If our salvation is kept for us, then it cannot be lost. So, who keeps it?" asked Bro. John.

Paul chimed in and said, "Well, the words following say that it is by God's power that we are kept."

"That's right," said Bro. John. "God keeps us by His power. Therefore, He actually preserves our salvation so we will persevere. Does that make sense to you men?" he asked.

"Let me see if I can repeat it back to you so it makes sense to me, if that's okay?" Linden asked.

"Sure thing, give it a shot, Linden," replied Bro. John.

"Okay, here goes," replied Linden. "We persevere in our faith in our Lord because God preserves our faith in the Lord."

"Very good, Linden!" exclaimed Bro. John. "Now, men, I want you to put on your thinking caps. Over the last couple of weeks, we discussed many things concerning God—His divine election, His sovereignty, and so forth. Think about God's election. How does the preservation of the saints by God relate to election?"

The men thought for a moment, and Dennis finally broke the silence. "I have a thought, Bro. John" said Dennis. "You taught us that

God accomplishes all that He set out to do. We saw from the scripture that nothing can thwart God's will and purpose. So, if God elects people to salvation, then the election was ordained by Him. Nothing can take away the election. Therefore, it is set, or as we just read in 1 Peter, it is kept for us by the power of God. We cannot undo what God has done."

Bro. John, upon the response from Dennis, immediately shot his hand into the air toward Dennis for a high five. Dennis responded with an enthusiastic slap.

"Very good, Dennis," Bro. John replied. "That is exactly right. To lose our salvation would mean that God would have to declare the election of His elect null and void. Yet, He will not do that. In fact, the Apostle Paul gives us a great statement of the preservation of our salvation in Romans 8:35-39. Turn to that passage if you would because these verses declare how God preserves us."

The men turned to Romans 8, and Bro. John asked Linden if he would read it aloud for the men. Linden cleared his throat and read the following:

> "Who shall separate us from the love of Christ? Shall tribulation, or distress, or persecution, or famine, or nakedness, or danger, or sword? As it is written, "For your sake we are being killed all the day long; we are regarded as sheep to be slaughtered." No, in all these things we are more than conquerors through him who loved us. For I am sure that neither death nor life, nor angels nor rulers, nor things present nor things to come, nor powers, nor height nor depth, nor anything else in all creation, will be able to separate us from the love of God in Christ Jesus our Lord." (Romans 8:35-39)

After Linden finished reading the passage, Bro. John asked Dennis if he would turn to Philippians 1:6 and read it aloud to the group. Dennis quickly found the passage and read,

> "And I am sure of this, that he who began a good work in you will bring it to completion at the day of Jesus Christ." (Philippians 1:6)

Bro. John looked around at the men gathered at the table and asked, "Men, if God accomplishes His purpose in all things and He has stated through the scriptures that nothing can ever separate us from His love, then can we ever be separated from God?"

"Not at all," responded Juan. "In fact, what Dennis just read is one of my favorite verses. God completes what He starts. So, if He elected me from the foundation of the world, then He will keep me until He calls me home."

The men nodded in agreement as Bro. John said, "Men, here it is in a nutshell: Our confidence in our salvation does not rest in our will. It rests with God's sovereign grace. I would much rather trust in Him than in myself."

"I agree, pastor," said Paul, "but what do the non-reformists say about this doctrine?"

Bro. John responded by saying, "There are some in the non-reformist camp who do believe in the perseverance of the saints. However, those who are in the camp that say you can lose your salvation say that God will not force perseverance upon a person because He never violates their will. They can make a choice toward losing their salvation as well as a choice for salvation because of their free will. The reformed believer, however, believes that God works in us, with our wills. Therefore, the believer will persevere. We cannot unjustify what has been justified. Some in the opposite camp tell us that certain sins will cause us to lose our salvation. Yet, if we say that our sins will cause us to be lost, then we have declared that the power of sin is greater than the power of God in keeping us for eternity. Make sense?" asked Bro. John.

"Perfect sense to me," responded Paul.

The men nodded in agreement, and Bro. John continued as he took the watch from the table and placed it carefully in his pocket. "Now that you persevered through this discussion this morning, would you like to continue our discussion about why this matters?"

"Absolutely," remarked Dennis. "Besides, if I go home now, it's honey-do time, so keep talking."

The men, who were keenly aware of what that statement entailed, chuckled, each taking another sip of coffee and discussing what lay ahead of each of them when they returned home. After he listened to the tasks awaiting them at home, Bro. John said, "Well, knowing that you are chomping at the bits to get home, let me continue our discussion."

"Please," said Dennis, "take your time!"

Chapter Thirteen

WHY DOES IT MATTER?

"Let's ask the question: Why does this matter?" said Bro. John. "In light of the fact that God is not obligated to save anyone but in His infinite and sovereign grace chose to do so, how does that affect your life with God?"

Dennis quickly responded and said, "I don't know about the other men, but as for me, I am absolutely humbled at the fact that God would choose me."

"So, you see this doctrine as a means of humbling you before God?" asked Bro. John.

"That's right," replied Dennis. "I know I am a sinner who would not choose God, had He not intervened in my life. When I see my sinfulness as compared to who He is, I have nothing to brag about."

"So, this doctrine matters because it moves us to humility like no other doctrine does, correct?" inquired Bro. John.

The men agreed, and Paul responded, "I think it matters because it emphasizes the sovereignty of God."

"So, what does it matter?" asked Bro. John in order to play the devil's advocate.

"It matters greatly in the fact that God says He only is to receive glory. If I can say I had something to do with my election, then I share in the sovereign role and have to receive some of the glory myself or perhaps even become more sovereign than God because I have the final decision if I am going to accept or reject Him," countered Paul.

"Very good, Paul!" exclaimed Br. John. "Now is there any practical application to the doctrine of the sovereignty of God?" asked the pastor.

"Less complaining," remarked Juan.

"How is that?" queried Bro. John.

"It's simple really, pastor. When you know that God is in control of everything, then when events, situations, or anything else happens, you know that He must have allowed it to happen. If He allows it to happen or not to happen, then you see these things from a different perspective. There is no need to complain because you know a sovereign God is in control. You can believe that they happened for a purpose so you now bow in submission to His plan and move forward in life with less complaining about circumstances," answered Juan.

"Okay, I see," said Linden. "It's a lesson in submission."

"Yes," replied Juan. "I have learned submission in a whole new light since I embraced these doctrines."

"What about you, Bro. John?" asked Linden. "Why does this matter to you as a pastor?"

"Glad you asked, Linden," remarked Bro. John. "I want you guys to remember these three words that were told to me many years ago by a godly pastor and mentor." He then said,

"Doctrine determines direction."

"What do you mean, sir?" asked Dennis.

"Let me give you an example," answered Bro. John. "Suppose I believed that there was not only one way to God. You could come other ways as long as they reach the same God who we all worship anyway just in different forms and fashion. How would you suppose I would lead a congregation?"

The men thought for a moment, and then Linden answered, "You wouldn't be preaching that the Bible is literally true. I know that for a fact, because Jesus says He is the only way to God."

"Exactly," responded Bro. John. "In fact, I might question the whole Bible and teach it as a good example to follow, but in the end, you would determine your destiny because there are many ways to God, so you would get to choose your own way. That means that I would allow all kinds of teaching to go on in my congregation. Yet you know that is not my doctrine. The doctrine I hold to determines how I preach, how I teach, and how I present the gospel. My doctrine determines my direction in how I would lead the church, what I would allow to be taught in the church, and what I would allow to take place in the church. So the doctrine of election has tremendous impact on the way we do church. For example, I would not and do not spend time on giving emotional appeals or talk about the free will of man in the sense that he has the last choice. Nor do I preach about self-esteem or preach a man-centered gospel. I know that we are all depraved and that without God intervening, we would all perish. So man must see who he is in contrast to a holy God. Therefore, I preach according to the doctrines I hold. So, practically, the doctrine of election matters greatly, for with your doctrine comes your direction."

"I never thought of it that way," replied Dennis, "but now that I think about it, the church we attend does the same thing. It follows a path determined by the doctrine it holds."

"You're right, Dennis," said Bro. John. "Examine why you do the things you do and why your church does what it does, and you will see that what you and they believe will be worked out in its practice."

"Well, my doctrine that says it's time to eat is determining that we order breakfast! So, I vote we follow my doctrine and order! I'm starving!" quipped Paul as he motioned for the waitress.

The men laughed at Paul's doctrine but determined that they were hungry too, so they joined him in ordering. After they enjoyed their breakfast and their conversation, Bro. John pulled out four folders from his briefcase, handed them to the men, and said, "Men, these are the scripture references I promised you as well as a list of books that you might want to read as you continue to study these doctrines. Remember that Rome wasn't conquered in a day and you will not grasp all that these teachings contain in a day either. So, read through them as you have time, study the books if you choose to get them, and determine if what they say is true according to the scripture."

"Bro. John," said Linden, "I know I can't thank you enough for taking the time to talk with us these past few weeks. I must confess that this doctrine has indeed spurned such an interest in me that I have been absorbed in study, which has opened my eyes to so much. And like you said, it has turned my life upside down!"

"You're welcome, Linden. It was my pleasure. I am always eager to share with those who are truly inquiring about the doctrine of election. If I can be of any further assistance in the future, please don't hesitate to call. I will try to answer any questions you have," replied Bro. John. "That goes for each of you."

As the men left the table, they each embraced the pastor, thanked him once again, and moved toward the parking lot. After they said good-bye to Bro. John, Dennis turned to Linden and asked, "Well, what are your thoughts after these meetings, my friend?"

"My thoughts?" responded Linden. "To sum it up, my heart is inclined to be a Calvinist!"

Chapter Fourteen

A NEW JOURNEY

Five months passed since Bro. John had met with Linden, Dennis, Juan, and Paul. He had taken a few calls from them over the months as they had questions concerning the doctrines of grace, but he had not heard from them in about two months. He often wondered if they had continued their study and what conclusions they had reached concerning all they had discussed.

On one brisk Sunday morning as he entered the sanctuary, as was his usual routine to greet his flock and visitors before the service was to start, he was met by his secretary, who informed him that he had some visitors waiting to meet him. She led him to the fourth pew where, much to his surprise, he saw Linden and Dennis sitting with their wives.

"My goodness, it's great to see you guys!" blurted Bro. John. "Did you get lost on the way to your church this morning?"

The men stood up quickly, shook hands with Bro. John, and began the introductions of their wives.

"Bro. John, this is my wife, Diana," Linden said. "She has been anxious to meet you."

"Good morning, Diana. It is good to meet the better half!" responded Bro. John.

"So you're the one who has corrupted my husband," teased Diana.

"No, he was already corrupted when I met him," replied Bro. John jokingly.

Bro. John turned to the woman sitting by Dennis's side and said, "You must be the better half of Dennis. I'm Bro. John."

Dennis quickly interjected, "This is my wife, Sue. Unlike Diana, she knew I was already corrupted before we met!"

They laughed as Bro. John asked, "What brings you to Sovereign Bible Church this fine morning?"

Linden spoke and said, "Bro. John, remember how you said in our last meeting together that doctrine determines direction?"

"Yes," replied the pastor.

"Well, Dennis, Juan, Paul, and I continued to meet to discuss what we were reading and studying about the doctrine of election. We have moved from being inclined toward Calvinism to a full embracing of the doctrines. We do not have all the answers and probably never will, but because our doctrine has changed, so has our direction. Dennis and I have been explaining these doctrines to our wives, and they have fully embraced them also. So, since doctrine determines direction, we wanted to visit and see where God may be leading us."

"Now, guys, it wasn't my intent to get you to change churches when we were meeting together. I hope you know that," stated Bro. John.

"We know, pastor," said Linden. "But since we have embraced these doctrines, we want to sit under teaching that continues to strengthen us and help us understand more completely God's sovereignty and His grace. We believe your church is the place."

"We are grateful to have you visiting with us, my friends," declared Bro. John. "I do hope you receive a blessing from the Lord this morning."

As Bro. John excused himself to greet more visitors, the couples sat down in the pew to await the beginning of the service. Dennis leaned over from his seat and said to Linden, "Well, this is a new direction."

Linden smiled and replied, "More like a new journey, my friend, a new journey."

Concerning the Sovereignty of God

"Remember the former things of old; for I am God, and there is no other; I am God, and there is none like me, declaring the end from the beginning and from ancient times things not yet done, saying, 'My counsel shall stand, and I will accomplish all my purpose,' calling a bird of prey from the east, the man of my counsel from a far country. I have spoken, and I will bring it to pass; I have purposed, and I will do it." **(Isaiah 46:9-11)**

"Our God is in the heavens; he does all that he pleases" **(Psalm 115:3).**

"But he is unchangeable, and who can turn him back? What he desires, that he does" **(Job 23:13).**

"O LORD, God of our fathers, are you not God in heaven? You rule over all the kingdoms of the nations. In your hand are power and might, so that none is able to withstand you" **(2 Chronicles 20:6).**

"For this is what the promise said: 'About this time next year I will return, and Sarah shall have a son.' And not only so, but also when Rebekah had conceived children by one man, our forefather Isaac, though they were not yet born and had done nothing either good or bad—in order that God's purpose of election might continue, not because of works but because of him who calls—she was told, 'The older will serve the younger.' As it is written, 'Jacob I loved, but Esau I hated.' What shall we say then? Is there injustice on God's part? By no means! For he says to Moses, 'I will have mercy on whom I have mercy, and I will have compassion on whom I have compassion.' So then it depends not on human will or exertion, but on God, who has mercy." **(Romans 9:9-16)**

"Whatever the LORD pleases, he does, in heaven and on earth, in the seas and all deeps." **(Psalm 135:6)**

"I know that you can do all things, and that no purpose of yours can be thwarted." **(Job 42:2)**

"So shall my word be that goes out from my mouth; it shall not return to me empty, but it shall accomplish that which I purpose, and shall succeed in the thing for which I sent it." **(Isaiah 55:11)**

"All the inhabitants of the earth are accounted as nothing, and he does according to his will among the host of heaven and among the inhabitants of the earth; and none can stay his hand or say to him, 'What have you done?" **(Daniel 4:35)**

"The LORD of hosts has sworn: 'As I have planned, so shall it be, and as I have purposed, so shall it stand' . . . For the LORD of hosts has purposed, and who will annul it? His hand is stretched out, and who will turn it back?"
(Isaiah 14:24,27)

"Does a bird fall in a snare on the earth, when there is no trap for it? Does a snare spring up from the ground, when it has taken nothing? Is a trumpet blown in a city, and the people are not afraid? Does disaster come to a city, unless the LORD has done it?" **(Amos 3:5-6)**

"For the Lord will not cast off forever, but, though He cause grief, He will have compassion according to the abundance of his steadfast love; for He does not willingly afflict or grieve the children of men. To crush underfoot all the prisoners of the earth, to deny a man justice in the presence of the Most High, to subvert a man in his lawsuit, the Lord does not approve. Who has spoken and it came to pass, unless the Lord has commanded it? Is it not from the mouth of the Most High that good and bad come?" **(Lamentations 3:31-38)**

"But who are you, O man, to answer back to God? Will what is molded say to its molder, 'Why have you made me like this?' Has the potter no right over the clay, to make out of the same lump one vessel for honorable use and another for dishonorable use?" **(Romans 9:21)**

"In him we have obtained an inheritance, having been predestined according to the purpose of him who works all things according to the counsel of his will." **(Ephesians 1:11)**

"And Jesus came and said to them, 'All authority in heaven and on earth has been given to me." **(Matthew 28:18)**

Concerning the Fallen Condition and Inability of Man

"But of the tree of the knowledge of good and evil you shall not eat, for in the day that you eat of it you shall surely die." **(Genesis 2:17)**

"Therefore, just as sin came into the world through one man, and death through sin, and so death spread to all men because all sinned—" **(Romans 5:12)**

"And you were dead in the trespasses and sins in which you once walked, following the course of this world, following the prince of the power of the air, the spirit that is now at work in the sons of disobedience— among whom we all once lived in the passions of our flesh, carrying out the desires of the body and the mind, and were by nature children of wrath, like the rest of mankind." **(Ephesians 2:1-3)**

"Remember that you were at that time separated from Christ, alienated from the commonwealth of Israel and strangers to the covenants of promise, having no hope and without God in the world." **(Ephesians 2:12)**

"The Lord saw that the wickedness of man was great in the earth, and that every intention of the thoughts of his heart was only evil continually." **(Genesis 6:5)**

"Behold, I was brought forth in iniquity, and in sin did my mother conceive me." **(Psalm 51:5)**

"As it is written: 'None is righteous, no, not one; no one understands; no one seeks for God. All have turned aside; together they have become worthless; no one does good, not even one." **(Romans 3:10-12)**

"For the mind that is set on the flesh is hostile to God, for it does not submit to God's law; indeed, it cannot. Those who are in the flesh cannot please God." **(Romans 8:7-8)**

"We have all become like one who is unclean, and all our righteous deeds are like a polluted garment. We all fade like a leaf, and our iniquities, like the wind, take us away."
(Isaiah 64:6)

"The natural person does not accept the things of the Spirit of God, for they are folly to him, and he is not able to understand them because they are spiritually discerned."
(1 Corinthians 2:14)

"And this is the judgment: the light has come into the world, and people loved the darkness rather than the light because their works were evil."
(John 3:19)

"Why do you not understand what I say? It is because you cannot bear to hear my word. You are of your father the devil, and your will is to do your father's desires. He was a murderer from the beginning, and has nothing to do with the truth, because there is no truth in him. When he lies, he speaks out of his own character, for he is a liar and the father of lies. But because I tell the truth, you do not believe me."
(John 8:43-45)

"No one can come to me unless the Father who sent me draws him. And I will raise him up on the last day." **(John 6:44)**

"For all have sinned and fall short of the glory of God."
(Romans 3:23)

"We have all become like one who is unclean, and all our righteous deeds are like a polluted garment. We all fade like a leaf, and our iniquities, like the wind, take us away."
(Isaiah 64:6)

Concerning God's Unconditional Election

"Even as he chose us in him before the foundation of the world, that we should be holy and blameless before him. In love—" **(Ephesians 1:4)**

"Though they were not yet born and had done nothing either good or bad—in order that God's purpose of election might continue, not because of works but because of him who calls—she was told, 'The older will serve the younger.' As it is written, 'Jacob I loved, but Esau I hated." **(Romans 9:11-13)**

"For he says to Moses, 'I will have mercy on whom I have mercy, and I will have compassion on whom I have compassion.' So then it depends not on human will or exertion, but on God, who has mercy."
(Romans 9:15-16)

"And when the Gentiles heard this, they began rejoicing and glorifying the word of the Lord, and as many as were appointed to eternal life believed." **(Acts 13:48)**

"But we ought always to give thanks to God for you, brothers beloved by the Lord, because God chose you as the first fruits to be saved, through sanctification by the Spirit and belief in the truth." **(2 Thessalonians 2:13)**

"And he will send out his angels with a loud trumpet call, and they will gather his elect from the four winds, from one end of heaven to the other." **(Matthew 24:31)**

"And if the Lord had not cut short the days, no human being would be saved. But for the sake of the elect, whom he chose, he shortened the days." **(Mark 13:20)**

"But you are a chosen race, a royal priesthood, a holy nation, a people for his own possession, that you may proclaim the excellencies of him who called you out of darkness into his marvelous light." **(1 Peter 2:9)**

"You did not choose me, but I chose you and appointed you that you should go and bear fruit and that your fruit should abide, so that whatever you ask the Father in my name, he may give it to you." **(John 15:16)**

"And all who dwell on earth will worship it, everyone whose name has not been written before the foundation of the world in the book of life of the Lamb who was slain." **(Revelation 13:8)**

"Behold, to the LORD your God belong heaven and the heaven of heavens, the earth with all that is in it. 15 Yet the LORD set his heart in love on your fathers and chose their offspring after them, you above all peoples, as you are this day." **(Deuteronomy 10:14-15)**

"Blessed is the one you choose and bring near, to dwell in your courts! We shall be satisfied with the goodness of your house, the holiness of your temple!" **(Psalm 65:4)**

"All things have been handed over to me by my Father, and no one knows the Son except the Father, and no one knows the Father except the Son and anyone to whom the Son chooses to reveal him." **(Matthew 11:27)**

"For many are called, but few are chosen." **(Matthew 11:27)**

"But God chose what is foolish in the world to shame the wise; God chose what is weak in the world to shame the strong; God chose what is low and despised in the world, even things that are not, to bring to nothing things that are, so that no human being might boast in the presence of God." **(1 Corinthians 1:27-29)**

Concerning Particular Redemption

"She will bear a son, and you shall call his name Jesus, for he will save his people from their sins." **(Matthew 1:21)**

"Even as the Son of Man came not to be served but to serve, and to give his life as a ransom for many." **(Matthew 20:28)**

"I am the good shepherd. The good shepherd lays down his life for the sheep." **(John 10:11)**

"To him the gatekeeper opens. The sheep hear his voice, and he calls his own sheep by name and leads them out. When he has brought out all his own, he goes before them, and the sheep follow him, for they know his voice." **(John 10:3-4)**

"I am the good shepherd. I know my own, and my own know me." **(John 10:14)**

"For those whom he foreknew he also predestined to be conformed to the image of his Son, in order that he might be the firstborn among many brothers. And those whom he predestined he also called, and those whom he called he also justified, and those whom he justified he also glorified."
(Romans 8:29-30)

"He who did not spare his own Son but gave him up for us all, how will he not also with him graciously give us all things? Who shall bring any charge against God's elect? It is God who justifies."
(Romans 8:32-33)

"All that the Father gives me will come to me, and whoever comes to me I will never cast out. For I have come down from heaven, not to do my own will but the will of him who sent me. And this is the will of him who sent me, that I should lose nothing of all that he has given me, but raise it up on the last day." **(John 6:37-39)**

"Therefore he is the mediator of a new covenant, so that those who are called may receive the promised eternal inheritance, since a death has occurred that redeems them from the transgressions committed under the first covenant." **(Hebrews 9:15)**

"And they sang a new song, saying, 'Worthy are you to take the scroll and to open its seals, for you were slain, and by your blood you ransomed people for God from every tribe and language and people and nation." **(Revelation 5:9)**

"For this is my blood of the covenant, which is poured out for many for the forgiveness of sins." **(Matthew 26:28)**

"When Jesus had spoken these words, he lifted up his eyes to heaven, and said, 'Father, the hour has come; glorify your Son that the Son may glorify you, since you have given him authority over all flesh, to give eternal life to all whom you have given him. And this is eternal life, that they know you the only true God, and Jesus Christ whom you have sent." **(John 17:1-3)**

"I am praying for them. I am not praying for the world but for those whom you have given me, for they are yours. All mine are yours, and yours are mine, and I am glorified in them. And I am no longer in the world, but they are in the world, and I am coming to you. Holy Father, keep them in your name, which you have given me, that they may be one, even as we are one." **(John 17: 9-11)**

"For it has been granted to you that for the sake of Christ you should not only believe in him but also suffer for his sake." **(Philippians 1:29)**

"For we know, brothers loved by God, that he has chosen you, because our gospel came to you not only in word, but also in power and in the Holy Spirit and with full conviction. You know what kind of men we proved to be among you for your sake." **(1 Thessalonians 1:4-5)**

Concerning the Effective Call of God

"Since you have been born again, not of perishable seed but of imperishable, through the living and abiding word of God." **(1 Peter 2:23)**

"And the Lord your God will circumcise your heart and the heart of your offspring, so that you will love the Lord your God with all your heart and with all your soul, that you may live."
(Deuteronomy 30:6)

"And I will give you a new heart, and a new spirit I will put within you. And I will remove the heart of stone from your flesh and give you a heart of flesh. And I will put my Spirit within you, and cause you to walk in my statutes and be careful to obey my rules." **(Ezekiel 36:26-27)**

"For as the Father raises the dead and gives them life, so also the Son gives life to whom He will." **(John 5:21)**

"All that the Father gives me will come to me, and whoever comes to me I will never cast out. No one can come to me unless the Father who sent me draws him. And I will raise him up on the last day. It is written in the Prophets, 'And they will all be taught by God.' Everyone who has heard and learned from the Father comes to me."
(John 6:37, 44-45)

"But there are some of you who do not believe." (For Jesus knew from the beginning who those were who did not believe, and who it was who would betray him.) And he said, 'This is why I told you that no one can come to me unless it is granted him by the Father." **(John 6:64-65)**

"At that time Jesus declared, 'I thank you, Father, Lord of heaven and earth, that you have hidden these things from the wise and understanding and revealed them to little children; yes, Father, for such was your gracious will. All things have been handed over to me by my Father, and no one knows the Son except the Father, and no one knows the Father except the Son and anyone to whom the Son chooses to reveal him." **(Matthew 11:25-27)**

"But to all who did receive him, who believed in his name, he gave the right to become children of God, who were born, not of blood nor of the will of the flesh nor of the will of man, but of God." **(John 1:12-13)**

"And you, who were dead in your trespasses and the uncircumcision of your flesh, God made alive together with him, having forgiven us all our trespasses." **(Colossians 2:13)**

"Even when we were dead in our trespasses, made us alive together with Christ—by grace you have been saved." **(Ephesians 2:5)**

"And those whom he predestined he also called, and those whom he called he also justified, and those whom he justified he also glorified." **(Romans 8:30)**

"In order to make known the riches of his glory for vessels of mercy, which he has prepared beforehand for glory—even us whom he has called, not from the Jews only but also from the Gentiles?" **(Romans 9:23-24)**

"Paul, called by the will of God to be an apostle of Christ Jesus, and our brother Sosthenes, To the church of God that is in Corinth, to those sanctified in Christ Jesus, called to be saints together with all those who in every place call upon the name of our Lord Jesus Christ, both their Lord and ours." **(1 Corinthians 1:1-2)**

"His divine power has granted to us all things that pertain to life and godliness, through the knowledge of him who called us to his own glory and excellence." **(2 Peter 1:3)**

"Jude, a servant of Jesus Christ and brother of James, To those who are called, beloved in God the Father and kept for Jesus Christ." **(Jude 1)**

Concerning Security in Him

"My sheep hear my voice, and I know them, and they follow me. I give them eternal life, and they will never perish, and no one will snatch them out of my hand. My Father, who has given them to me, is greater than all, and no one is able to snatch them out of the Father's hand. I and the Father are one." **(John 10:27-30)**

"Truly, truly, I say to you, whoever hears my word and believes him who sent me has eternal life. He does not come into judgment, but has passed from death to life." **(John 5:24)**

"In him you also, when you heard the word of truth, the gospel of your salvation, and believed in him, were sealed with the promised Holy Spirit, who is the guarantee of our inheritance until we acquire possession of it, to the praise of his glory." **(Ephesians 1:13-14)**

"And do not grieve the Holy Spirit of God, by whom you were sealed for the day of redemption." **(Ephesians 4:30)**

"For God so loved the world, that he gave his only Son, that whoever believes in him should not perish but have eternal life." (John 3:16)

"But God shows his love for us in that while we were still sinners, Christ died for us. Since, therefore, we have now been justified by his blood, much more shall we be saved by him from the wrath of God. For if while we were enemies we were reconciled to God by the death of his Son, much more, now that we are reconciled, shall we be saved by his life."
(Romans 5:8-10)

"For I am sure that neither death nor life, nor angels nor rulers, nor things present nor things to come, nor powers, nor height nor depth, nor anything else in all creation, will be able to separate us from the love of God in Christ Jesus our Lord." **(Romans 8:38-39)**

"He entered once for all into the holy places, not by means of the blood of goats and calves but by means of his own blood, thus securing an eternal redemption. Therefore he is the mediator of a new covenant, so that those who are called may receive the promised eternal inheritance, since a death has occurred that redeems them from the transgressions committed under the first covenant." **(Hebrews 9:12,15)**

"For you have died, and your life is hidden with Christ in God. When Christ who is your life appears, then you also will appear with him in glory." **(Colossians 3:3-4)**

"I will make with them an everlasting covenant, that I will not turn away from doing good to them. And I will put the fear of me in their hearts, that they may not turn from me."
(Jeremiah 32:40)

"For the mountains may depart and the hills be removed, but my steadfast love shall not depart from you, and my covenant of peace shall not be removed,' says the LORD, who has compassion on you."
(Isaiah 54:10)

"What do you think? If a man has a hundred sheep, and one of them has gone astray, does he not leave the ninety-nine on the mountains and go in search of the one that went astray? And if he finds it, truly, I say to you, he rejoices over it more than over the ninety-nine that never went astray. So it is not the will of my Father who is in heaven that one of these little ones should perish." **(Matthew 18:12-14)**

"Blessed be the God and Father of our Lord Jesus Christ! According to his great mercy, he has caused us to be born again to a living hope through the resurrection of Jesus Christ from the dead, to an inheritance that is imperishable, undefiled, and unfading, kept in heaven for you, who by God's power are being guarded through faith for a salvation ready to be revealed in the last time." **(1 Peter 1:3-5)**

"Knowing that he who raised the Lord Jesus will raise us also with Jesus and bring us with you into his presence." **(2 Corinthians 4:14)**

"Jude, a servant of Jesus Christ and brother of James, To those who are called, beloved in God the Father and kept for Jesus Christ." **(Jude 1)**

Total Depravity: Man's nature is corrupt and sinful. The word "total" does not mean that man is as evil as he can be. Even the most hardened criminal can be nice every once in a while! The word "total" means that man's whole being, everything that makes up his nature, is affected by sin. Because of this, a person in his or her sinful state is unable to do anything that is spiritually good. That person is enslaved to sin. He is unable to save himself.

Inability: When the Calvinist uses this term, he means that man, because of his sinful nature, does not have the ability to even come to Christ. He does not have the spiritual ability to do anything that would pertain to his salvation. To put it another way, man does not have the ability to choose God because he is unwilling to do so because of his fallen state.

Unconditional Election: God, in His sovereignty and before the foundation of the world, chose individuals from fallen humanity as the objects of His grace and mercy. These individuals He has purposed to save. His election of these individuals is not based on anything in the individuals or a foreseen response by those elected but on the basis of God's pleasure and will.

Limited Atonement: This term can get confusing to the "incliner." Some may think that this term means that God's power is limited in the atonement. However, this is not the case. The Calvinist believes that the atonement of Christ is unlimited in its power but is limited to those God chooses to save. Calvinists also believe that when Christ comes to save His people, He actually does save them and removes the guilt of their sins from them. Yet the number of those chosen is limited.

Irresistible Grace: When God chooses to save someone, then God will accomplish His purpose in the chosen's life. In that way, when God sends His Holy Spirit to save the individual, no one can resist Him. The term does not mean that the individual is forced against his or her will to do something that he or she does not want to do. When God sends His Holy Spirit to a person, the person is changed in his or her heart and character, and that person is now truly sorry for his or her sins and desires God. He or she freely seeks after God.

Perseverance of the Saints: Those who have been called, justified, and redeemed by God are kept in faith by God Himself. Nothing can separate them from the love of God. True believers do, at times, fall into temptations and commit sin, but these do not cause them to lose their salvation. God will bring those who have drifted away through sin back to Him through various means.

Free Will: The Calvinist defines free will as "the mind choosing" and "choosing what we want" according to our strongest inclination at the moment. Motives, inclinations, and desires are shaped by the mind. Therefore, our choices or acts of the will are determined by our desires.

Moral Ability: This is the ability to make a choice for Christ. For the Calvinist, man in his fallen state does not have the ability to choose Christ. Man does not have the ability because his nature is corrupt and he will only choose according to his desires. Fallen man does not have the desire for Christ. To sum it up, man does not have the moral ability within him to choose Christ.

Bro. John's Book List

Chosen by God. R. C. Sproul, Tyndale House Publishers.

The Mystery of the Holy Spirit. R. C. Sproul, Tyndale House Publishers.

Grace Unknown. R. C. Sproul, Baker Books.

The Five Points of Calvinism. David Steele, Curtis C. Thomas, S. Lance Quinn, P&R Publishing.

The Reformed Doctrine of Predestination. Lorraine Boettner, P&R Publishing.

Election and Free Will. Robert A. Peterson, P&R Publishing.

Systematic Theology. Wayne Grudem, Zondervan Book Company

Election: Love before Time. Kenneth Johns, P&R Publishing.

A Biblical Defense of Predestination. Dr. Kenneth L. Gentry, Jr., Apologetics Group.

About the Author

Anthony Dean has been in the ministry for over thirty-five years, serving in many different capacities from youth minister to senior pastor. He holds a master's of divinity degree. He has been married for thirty-two years, and he has two grown sons.